Big Data for Insurance Companies

Big Data, Artificial Intelligence and Data Analysis Set

coordinated by
Jacques Janssen

Volume 1

Big Data for Insurance Companies

Edited by

Marine Corlosquet-Habart
Jacques Janssen

iSTE

WILEY

First published 2018 in Great Britain and the United States by ISTE Ltd and John Wiley & Sons, Inc.

ISTE Ltd
27-37 St George's Road
London SW19 4EU
UK

www.iste.co.uk

John Wiley & Sons, Inc.
111 River Street
Hoboken, NJ 07030
USA

www.wiley.com

Library of Congress Control Number: 2017959466

British Library Cataloguing-in-Publication Data
A CIP record for this book is available from the British Library
ISBN 978-1-78630-073-7

Contents

Foreword

Big data is not just a slogan, but a reality as shown by this book. Many companies and organizations in the fields of banking, insurance and marketing accumulate data but have not yet reaped the full benefits. Until then, statisticians could make these data more meaningful: through correlations and the search for major components. These methods provided interesting, sometimes important, but aggregated information.

The major innovation is that the power of computers now enables us to do two things that are completely different from what was done before:

– accumulate individual data on thousands or even millions of clients of a bank or insurance company, and even those who are not yet clients, and process them separately;

– deploy the massive use of unsupervised learning algorithms.

These algorithms, which, in principle, have been known for about 40 years, require computing power that was not available at that time and have since improved significantly. They are unsupervised, which means that from a broad set of behavioral data, they predict with amazing accuracy the subsequent decisions of an individual without knowing the determinants of his/her action.

In the first three chapters of this book, key experts in applied statistics and big data explain where the data come from and how they are used. The second and third chapters, in particular, provide details on the functioning of learning algorithms which are the basis of the spectacular results when using massive data. The fourth and fifth chapters are devoted to applications in the insurance sector. They are absolutely fascinating because they are written by highly skilled professionals who show that tomorrow's world is already here.

It is unnecessary to emphasize the economic impact of this study; the results obtained in detecting fraudsters are a tremendous reward to investments in massive data.

To the best of my knowledge, this is the first book that illustrates so well, in a professional context, the impact and real stakes of what some call the "big data revolution". Thus, I believe that this book will be a great success in companies.

Jean-Charles POMEROL
Chairman of the Scientific Board of ISTE Editions

Introduction

This book presents an overview of big data methods applied to insurance problems. Specifically, it is a multi-author book that gives a fairly complete view of five important aspects, each of which is presented by authors well known in the fields covered, who have complementary profiles and expertise (data scientists, actuaries, statisticians, engineers). These range from classical data analysis methods (including learning methods like *machine learning*) to the impact of *big data* on the present and future insurance market.

Big data, megadata or massive data apply to datasets that are so vast that not only the popular data management methods but also the classical methods of statistics (for example, inference) lose their meaning or cannot apply.

The exponential development of the power of computers linked to the crossroads of this data analysis with artificial intelligence helps us to initiate new analysis methods for gigantic databases that are mostly found in the insurance sector as presented in this book.

The first chapter, written by Romain Billot, Cécile Bothorel and Philippe Lenca (IMT Atlantique, Brest), presents a sound introduction to big data and its application to insurance. This chapter focuses on the impact of megadata, showing that hundreds of millions of people generate billions of bytes of data each day. The classical characterization of big data by 5Vs is well illustrated and enriched by other Vs such as variability and validity.

Introduction written by Marine CORLOSQUET-HABART and Jacques JANSSEN.

In order to remedy the insufficiency of classical data management techniques, the authors develop parallelization methods for data as well as possible tasks thanks to the development of computing via the parallelism of several computers.

The main IT tools, including Hadoop, are presented as well as their relationship with platforms specialized in decision-making solutions and the problem of migrating to a given oriented strategy. Application to insurance is tackled using three examples.

The second chapter, written by Gilbert Saporta (CNAM, Paris), reviews the transition from classical data analysis methods to big data, which shows how big data is indebted to data analysis and artificial intelligence, notably through the use of supervised or non-supervised learning methods. Moreover, the author emphasizes the methods for validating predictive models since it has been established that the ultimate goal for using big data is not only geared towards constituting gigantic and structured databases, but also and especially as a description and prediction tool from a set of given parameters.

The third chapter, written by Franck Vermet (EURIA, Brest), aims at presenting the most commonly used actuarial statistical learning methods applicable to many areas of life and non-life insurance. It also presents the distinction between supervised and non-supervised learning and the rigorous and clear use of neural networks for each of the methods, particularly the ones that are mostly used (decision trees, backpropagation of perceptron gradient, support vector machines, boosting, stacking, etc.).

The last two chapters are written by insurance professionals. In Chapter 4, Florence Picard (Institute of Actuaries, Paris) describes the present and future insurance market based on the development of big data. It illustrates its implementation in the insurance sector by particularly detailing the impact of big data on management methods, marketing and new insurable risks as well as data security. It pertinently highlights the emergence of new managerial techniques that reinforce the importance of continuous training.

Emmanuel Berthelé (Optimind Winter, Paris) is the author of the fifth and last chapter, who is also an actuary. He presents the main uses of big data in insurance, particularly pricing and product offerings, automobile and telematics insurance, index-based insurance, combating fraud and reinsurance. He also lays emphasis on the regulatory constraints specific to the sector

(Solvency II, ORSA, etc.) and the current restriction on the use of certain algorithms due to an audibility requirement, which will undoubtedly be uplifted in the future.

Finally, a fundamental observation emerges from these last two chapters cautioning insurers against preserving the mutualization principle which is the founding principle of insurance because as Emmanuel Berthelé puts it:

> "Even if the volume of data available and the capacities induced in the refinement of prices increase considerably, the personalization of price is neither fully feasible nor desirable for insurers, insured persons and society at large."

In conclusion, this book shows that big data is essential for the development of insurance as long as the necessary safeguards are put in place. Thus, this book is clearly addressed to insurance and bank managers as well as master's students in actuarial science, computer science, finance and statistics, and, of course, new master's students in big data who are currently increasing.

1

Introduction to Big Data and Its Applications in Insurance

1.1. The explosion of data: a typical day in the 2010s

At 7 am on a Monday like any other, a young employee of a large French company wakes up to start her week at work. As for many of us, technology has appeared everywhere in her daily life. As soon as she wakes up, her connected watch, which also works as a sports coach when she goes jogging or cycling, gives her a synopsis of her sleep quality and a score and assessment of the last few months. Data on her heartbeat measured by her watch are transmitted by WiFi to an app installed on her latest generation mobile, before her sleep cycles are analyzed to produce easy-to-handle quality indicators, like an overall score, and thus encourage fun and regular monitoring of her sleep. It is her best night's sleep for a while and she hurries to share her results by text with her best friend, and then on social media via Facebook and Twitter. In this world of connected health, congratulatory messages flood in hailing her "performance"! During her shower, online music streaming services such as Spotify or Deezer suggest a "wake-up" playlist, put together from the preferences and comments of thousands of users. She can give feedback on any of the songs for the software to adapt the

Chapter written by Romain BILLOT, Cécile BOTHOREL and Philippe LENCA.

upcoming songs in real time, with the help of a powerful recommendation system based on historical data. She enjoys her breakfast and is getting ready to go to work when the public transport Twitter account she subscribes to warns her of an incident causing serious disruption on the transport network. Hence, she decides to tackle the morning traffic by car, hoping to avoid arriving at work too late. To help her plan her route, she connects to a traffic information and community navigation app that obtains traffic information from GPS records generated by other drivers' devices throughout their journeys to update a real-time traffic information map. Users can flag up specific incidents on the transport network themselves, and our heroine marks slow traffic caused by an accident. She decides to take the alternative route suggested by the app. Having arrived at work, she vents her frustration at a difficult day's commute on social media. During her day at work, on top of her professional activity, she will be connected online to check her bank account balance and go shopping on a supermarket's "drive" app that lets her do her shop online and pick it up later in her car. Her consumer profile on the online shopping app gives her a historical overview of the last few months, as well as suggesting products that are likely to interest her. On her way home, the trunk full with food, some street art painted on a wall immediately attracts her attention. She stops to take a photo, edits it with a color filter and shares it on a social network similar to Instagram. The photo immediately receives about 10 "likes". That evening, a friend comments on the photo. Having recognized the artist, he gives her a link to an online video site like YouTube. The link is for a video of the street art being painted, put online by the artist to increase their visibility. She quickly watches it. Tired, she eats, plugs in her sleep app and goes to bed.

Between waking up and going to sleep, our heroine has generated a significant amount of data, a volume that it would have been difficult to imagine a few years earlier. With or without her knowledge, there have been hundreds of megabytes of data flow and digital records of her tastes, moods, desires, searches, location, etc. This *homo sapiens*, now *homo numericus*, is not alone – billions of us do the same. The figures are revealing and their growth astonishing: we have entered the era of big data. In 2016, one million links were shared, two million friend requests were made and three million messages were sent every 20 minutes on Facebook [STA 16a]. The figures are breathtaking:

- 1,540,000,000 users active at least once a month;
- 974,000,000 smartphone users;
- 12% growth in users between 2014 and 2015;
- 81 million Facebook profiles;
- 20 million applications installed on Facebook every day.

Since the start of computing, engineers and researchers have certainly been confronted with strong growth in data volumes, stored in larger and larger databases that have come to be known as data warehouses, and with ever improving architectures to guarantee high quality service. However, since the 2000s, mobile Internet and the Internet of Things, among other things, have brought about an explosion in data. This has been more or less well managed, requiring classical schemes to be reconsidered, both in terms of architecture and data processing. Internet traffic, computer backups on the cloud, shares on social networks, open data, purchase transactions, sensors and records from connected objects make up an assembly of markers in space and/or time of human activity, in all its dimensions. We produce enormous quantities of data and can produce it continuously wherever we are (the Internet is accessible from the office, home, airports, trains, cars, restaurants, etc.). In just a few clicks, you can, for example, describe and review a meal and send a photo of your dish. This great wealth of data certainly poses some questions, about ethics and security among other things, and also presents a great opportunity for society [BOY 12]. Uses of data that were previously hidden or reserved for an elite are becoming accessible to more and more people.

The same is true for the open data phenomenon establishing itself at all administrative scales. For big companies, and insurance companies in particular, there are multiple opportunities [CHE 12]. For example, data revealing driving styles are of interest to non-life insurance, and data concerning health and lifestyle are useful for life insurance. In both cases, knowing more about the person being insured allows better estimation of future risks. Storing this data requires a flexible and tailored architecture [ZIK 11] to allow parallel and dynamic processing of "voluminous", "varied" data at "velocity" while evaluating its "veracity" in order to derive the great "value" of these new data flows [WU 14]. Big data, or megadata, is often presented in terms of these five Vs.

After initial reflection on the origin of the term and with a view to giving a reliable definition (section 1.2), we will return to the framework of these five Vs, which has the advantage of giving a pragmatic overview of the characteristics of big data (section 1.3). Section 1.4 will describe current architecture models capable of real-time processing of high-volume and varied data, using parallel and distributed processing. Finally, we will finish with a succinct presentation of some examples from the world of insurance.

1.2. How is big data defined?

> "Big data is like teenage sex: everyone talks about it, nobody really knows how to do it, everyone thinks everyone else is doing it, so everyone claims they are doing it."
>
> Dan Ariely

It is difficult to define a term as generic, widely used and even clichéd as big data. According to Wikipedia[1]:

> "Big data is a term for datasets that are so large or complex that traditional data processing application software is inadequate to deal with them."

This definition of the big data phenomenon presents an interesting point of view. It focuses on the loss of capability of classical tools to process such high volumes of data. This point of view was put forward in a report from the consulting firm McKinsey and Company that describes big data as data whose scale, distribution, diversity and transience require new architectures and analysis techniques that can unlock new sources of value added [MAN 11]. Of course, this point of view prevails today (in 2016, as these lines are being written) and a universal definition must use more generic characteristics that

1 "Big Data", Wikipedia, The Free Encyclopedia, available at: https//en.wikipedia.org/wiki/Big_data, accessed 9th July 2017.

will stand the test of time. However, like many new concepts, there are as many definitions as there are authors on the subject. We refer the reader to [WAR 13] for an interesting discussion on this theme. To date the genesis of big data, why not make use of one of their greatest suppliers, the tech giant Google? Hence, we have extracted, with the help of the Google Trends tool, the growth in the number of searches for the term "big data" on the famous search engine. Figure 1.1 shows an almost exponential growth in the interest of people using the search engine from 2010 onwards, a sign of the youth of the term and perhaps a certain degree of surprise at a suddenly uncontrollable volume of data, as the Wikipedia definition, still relevant in 2016, suggests. However, articles have widely been using this concept since 1998, to relate a future development of data quantities and databases towards larger and larger scales [FAN 13, DIE 12]. The reference article, widely cited by the scientific community, dates from 2001 and is attributed to Doug Laney from the consultancy firm Gartner [LAN 01]. Curiously, the document never mentions the term big data, although it features the reference characterization of three Vs: *volume*, *velocity* and *variety*. "Volume" describes the size of the data, the term "velocity" captures the speed at which it is generated, communicated and must be processed, while the term "variety" refers to the heterogeneous nature of these new data flows. Most articles agree on the basic three Vs (see [FAN 13, FAN 14, CHE 14]), to which the fourth V of *veracity* (attributed to IBM [IBM 16]), as well as the fifth V, *value*, are added. The term "veracity" focuses on the reliability of the various data. Indeed, data can be erroneous, incomplete or too old for the intended analysis. The fifth V conveys the fact that data must above all create value for the companies involved, or society in general. In this respect, just as certain authors remind us that small volumes can create value ("small data also may lead to big value", see [GU 14]), we should not forget that companies, through adopting practices suited to big data, must most of all store, process and create *intelligent* data. Perhaps we should be talking about *smart data* rather than big data?

1.3. Characterizing big data with the five Vs

In our initial assessment of the big data phenomenon, it should be noted that the 3 Vs framework of volume, velocity and variety, popularized by the research firm Gartner [LAN 01], is now standard. We will thus start with this classical scheme, shown in Figure 1.2, before considering other Vs, which will soon prove to be useful for developing this initial description.

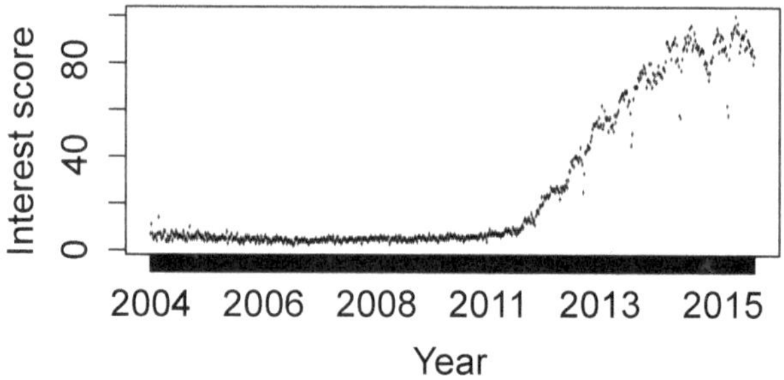

Figure 1.1. *Evolution of the interest in the term big data for Google searches (source: Google Trends, 27th September 2016)*

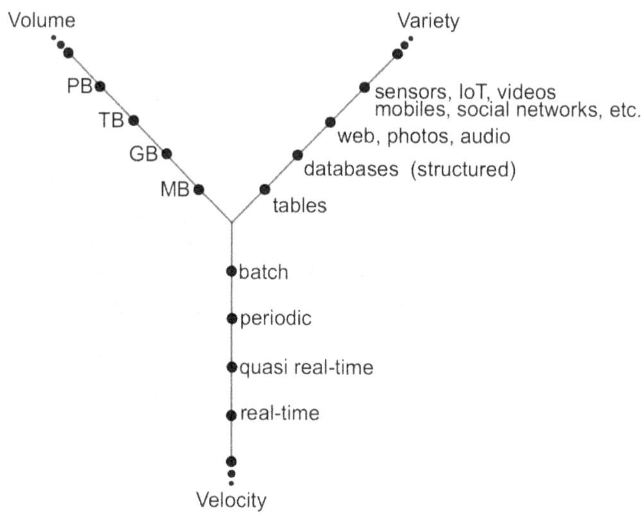

Figure 1.2. *The three Vs of big data*

1.3.1. *Variety*

In a break with tradition, we will start by focusing on the variety, rather than volume, of data. We refer here to the different types of data available today. As we illustrated in the introduction, data originates everywhere, for example:

– texts, photos and videos (Internet, etc.);

– spatio-temporal information (mobile devices, smart sensors, etc.);

– metadata on telephone messages and calls (mobile devices, etc.);

– medical information (patient databases, smart objects, etc.);

– astronomical and geographical data (satellites, ground-based observatories, etc.);

– client data (client databases, sensors and networked objects, etc.).

The handful of examples listed above illustrate the heterogeneity of sources and data – "classical" data like that seen before the era of big data, evidently, and also video signals, audio signals, metadata, etc.

This diversity of content has brought about an initial paradigm shift from structured to non-structured data. In the past, much data could be considered to be structured in the sense that they could be stored in relational databases. This was how client or commercial data was stored. Today, a large proportion of data is not structured (photos, video sequences, account updates, social network statuses, conversations, sensor data, recordings, etc.).

1.3.2. *Volume*

If you ask a range of different people to define big data, most of them will bring up the concept of size, volume or quantity. Just close your eyes and imagine the amount of messages, photos and videos exchanged per second globally. In parallel to the developing interest for the concept of big data on the search engine Google (Figure 1.1), Internet usage has also exploded in just a few years, as the annual number of Google searches bears witness (Table 1.1).

The explosion in Internet usage, and in particular mobile Internet as made possible by smartphones and high-speed standards, has led to an unstoppable growth in data volumes, towards units that our oldest readers have surely recently discovered: gigabytes, terabytes, petabytes, exabytes and even zettabytes (a zettabyte is 10^{21} bytes!), as shown in Figure 1.3.

Year	Annual number of searches	Average searches per day
2014	2,095,100,000,000	5,740,000,000
2013	2,161,530,000,000	5,922,000,000
2012	1,873,910,000,000	5,134,000,000
2011	1,722,071,000,000	4,717,000,000
2010	1,324,670,000,000	3,627,000,000
2009	953,700,000,000	2,610,000,000
2008	637,200,000,000	1,745,000,000
2007	438,000,000,000	1,200,000,000
2000	22,000,000,000	60,000,000
1998	3,600,000	9,800

Table 1.1. *Annual Google statistics [STA 16b]*

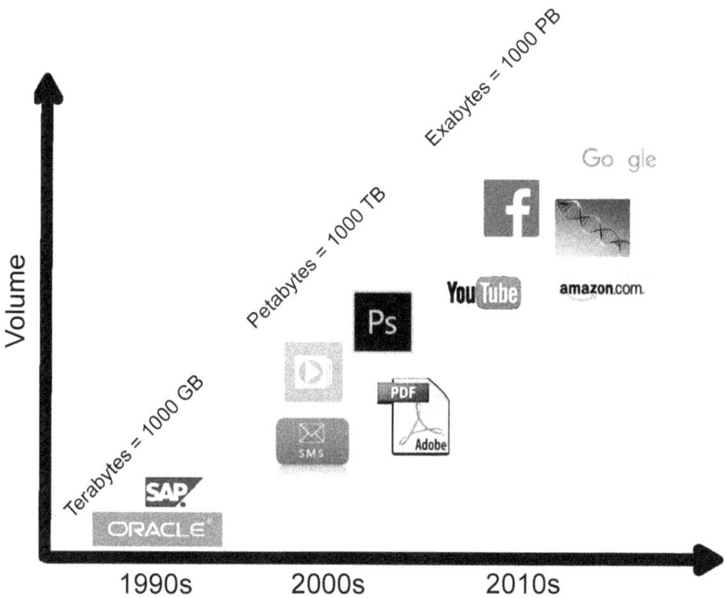

Figure 1.3. *Development of data volumes and their units of measure*

According to an annual report on the Internet of Things [GSM 15], by the end of 2015, there were 7.2 million mobile connections, with projections for smartphones alone reaching more than 7 million in 2019. This expansive volume of data is what brought forth the big data phenomenon. With current data stores unable to absorb such growth in data volumes, companies, engineers and researchers have had to create new solutions, notably offering distributed storage and processing of these masses of data (see section 1.4). The places that store this data, the famous data centers, also raise significant questions in terms of energetic consumption. One report highlights the fact that data centers handling American data consumed 91 billion kWh of electricity in 2013, equivalent to the annual output of 34 large coal-fired power plants [DEL 14]. This figure is likely to reach 140 billion in 2020, equivalent to the annual output of 50 power plants, costing the American population $13 billion per year in electricity bills. If we add to this the emission of 100 million metric tons of CO_2 per year, it is easy to see why large organizations have very quickly started taking this problem seriously, as demonstrated by the frequent installation of data centers in cold regions around the world, with ingenious systems for recycling natural energy [EUD 16].

1.3.3. *Velocity*

The last of the three historic Vs, the V for *velocity*, represents what would probably more naturally be called *speed*. It also covers multiple components, and it is intrinsic to the big data phenomenon. This is clear from the figures above regarding the development of the concept and volume of data, like a film in fast-forward. Speed can refer to the speed at which the data are generated, the speed at which they are transmitted and processed, and also the speed at which they can change form, provide value and, of course, disappear. Today, we must confront large waves of masses of data that must be processed in real time. This online-processed data allow decision makers to make strategic choices that they would not have even been aware of in the past.

1.3.4. *Towards the five Vs: veracity and value*

An enriched definition of big data quickly took shape with the appearance of a fourth element, the V of *veracity*, attributed to IBM [IBM 16]. The word veracity brings us back to the quality of the data, a vital property for all data search processes. Again, this concept covers different aspects, such as imprecision, incompleteness, inconsistency and uncertainty. According to IBM, poor data quality costs on average $3.1 trillion per year. The firm adds that 27% of questionnaire respondents are not sure of the information that they input and that one in three decision makers have doubts concerning the data they base their decision on. Indeed, the variety of data flows, which are often unstructured, complicates the process of certifying data. This brings to mind, for example, the quality of data on the social network Twitter, whose imposed 140 character format does not lend itself to precise prose that can be easily identified by automatic natural language processing tools. Certifying data is a prerequisite for creating value, which constitutes the fifth V that is well established in modern practices. The capacity to store, understand and analyze these new waves of high-volume, high-velocity, varied data, and to ensure reliability while integrating them into a *business intelligence* ecosystem, will undoubtedly allow all companies to put in place new decision advice modules (for example, predictive analysis) with high added value. One striking example concerns American sport and ticket sales that are currently based on dynamic pricing methods enhanced by historical and real-time data. Like many other American sports teams, the San Francisco Giants baseball team has thus adapted its match ticketing system to make use of big data. They engaged the services of the company QCUE to set up algorithmic trading techniques inspired by airline companies. The ticket prices are updated in real time as a function of supply and demand. In particular, historical data on the quality of matches and attendances are used to adjust ticket prices to optimize seat/stadium occupation and the company's profits. On their website, QCUE report potential profit growth of up to 46% compared to the previous system.

Globally, big data represents a lucrative business. The McKinsey Institute has suggested that even the simple use of client location data could yield a potential annual consumer surplus of $600 billion [MAN 11]. The consulting group Wikibon estimates that the big data market, encompassing hardware, software and related services, will grow from $19.6 billion in 2013 to $84 billion in 2026 [KEL 15].

1.3.5. *Other possible Vs*

Skimming through the immense number of articles dedicated to the subject, the reader soon realizes that each author is tempted to add their own personal V, each making their own contribution to the various aspects of big data. Thus, the terms variability and validity, which relate directly back to the previous concepts of variety and veracity, can also be added to the list. The word variability focuses on the versatile (yet another V!) nature of data, which can change over time, whereas validity is a more explicit reference to a certification process of classical data. Finally, without degenerating into unhelpful one-upmanship, it seems worthwhile to mention one last V, for visualization. The V of visibility is sometimes tied in with this. Big data, with all of its characteristics as described so far, calls for new forms of visualization to make the data understandable and presentable for decision makers. This can range from simple reporting tools offering an overarching view of the main data characteristics to more advanced methods combining visualization and data analysis. For example, visualization techniques with graphs demonstrating the complex relationships between contributors on social networks, clients, communities or naturally forming groups, are now commonplace.

1.4. Architecture

The era of big data is persuading enterprises of all sizes to implement processes to help make decisions based on data analysis. Predicting what will satisfy a client, optimizing processes and, more generally, generating value from data have now become essential for any business that wants to remain competitive. Although these have always been central challenges for insurers, they are no less affected by the more complex environment of the data economy. Growing volumes of data, of various different natures, with variable lifetimes and of disparate quality, which we want to interrogate in real time, are influencing the tools used, which continue to evolve.

We will see in this section that the scientific and technical environment is becoming richer and more complex by the day. New algorithms are dreamt up to address problems, and new tools are created to test and apply them. In this context, the main task for companies is to incorporate these innovations alongside existing tools in order to integrate new predictive data analysis processes with existing business procedures. This takes time and expertise, for the project to be defined, to get it running and then to maintain and update it.

1.4.1. *An increasingly complex technical ecosystem*

As has been mentioned already, the essence of the big data phenomenon lies in the limitation of "classical" tools and the need to upgrade them so that they can collect, store and analyze new types of ever greater volumes of data. As for data collection and storage, although all data combined together are usually high volume, each data source produces a "reasonable" volume that can still be managed by "classical" storage and analysis tools. An intelligent distribution of databases is often sufficient for the collection and storage of data in different physical servers, and if the need is felt to put them on the network, it is "sufficient" to use a distributed, robust and fault-tolerant storage system. Big data architectures are needed when each data source produces volumes incompatible with the analysis tools. We thus turn to parallelization, which expresses itself in two ways:

– data parallelism, where a single dataset is divided into subsets distributed over different machines;

– task parallelism, where the algorithms and different sub-procedures are executed concurrently on different processors.

Currently, the best-known big data architecture is probably Hadoop. Contrary to the myth attributing the creation of Hadoop to Yahoo, the project really started at Google. Doug Cutting was working on web content indexing there and needed a framework that would allow large numbers of operations to run in parallel over large collections of servers. The "MapReduce" principle of processing data spread over multiple servers, which is the programming model that Hadoop is based on, was published in 2004 by Google Labs. Doug Cutting joined Yahoo in 2008 and launched the first major Hadoop project, the Yahoo! Search Webmap, which runs on a cluster of 10,000 Linux cores. Today, Hadoop is an open source project managed by the Apache foundation [HAD 16], and its ecosystem is developing day by day with numerous projects optimizing or adding different components. In 2016, the major Web actors like Twitter and Facebook stored and searched through their tens of petabytes[2] of data on Hadoop.

The Hadoop *framework* can be broken down into three main modules:

– the Hadoop distributed file system (HDFS): the system of files is distributed over different nodes of a cluster. These data nodes are machines networked using a master-slave model. The machines themselves can be relatively modest (and hence inexpensive) servers, it is the number of them that guarantees the big data capacity of the cluster. Every file is split up into blocks. The blocks are distributed across several machines, which allow large volumes of files to be stored, including volumes exceeding the storage capacity of each of the servers. One particular node, the name node, tracks the location of the different blocks and allows access to the data. Each block is replicated at least three times over three different data nodes to ensure redundancy. This principle of horizontal distribution (sharding) enjoys the advantage of being easily re-scaled, since more data nodes can be added to increase the data storage capacity. Overall, HDFS is an efficient, fault-tolerant and scalable file system, which undoubtedly contributed substantially to its success;

– the MapReduce data processing engine: a MapReduce job (a processing task) is completed in two stages, a mapping step that transforms raw data into a key/value format, and a reducing step that combines all of the values for each of the keys. Data handling generally gives rise to a chain of several MapReduce jobs;

– the YARN (Yet Another Resource Negotiator) resource manager: this module was introduced in the second version of Hadoop and allows the infrastructure management to be completely dissociated from the MapReduce data processing model. Thus, while MapReduce describes the data manipulation processes, YARN calls on the name nodes and deals with launching these processes on the different data nodes. At the simplest level, YARN orchestrates the parallel management of the different processes to optimize the distribution of the processing work over the different machines.

2 1 PB (petabyte) = 1,000 TB (terabytes) = 1,000,000 GB (gigabytes).

A range of projects supplementing these core modules enhance the services provided to users, some of which are shown in Figure 1.4. Examples of these services include database management (Hbase) and searches (Hive), real-time data flow processing (Storm), high-level data manipulation scripts (Pig), Web interfaces facilitating data processing (Hue) and, of course, data analysis and search libraries (Mahout).

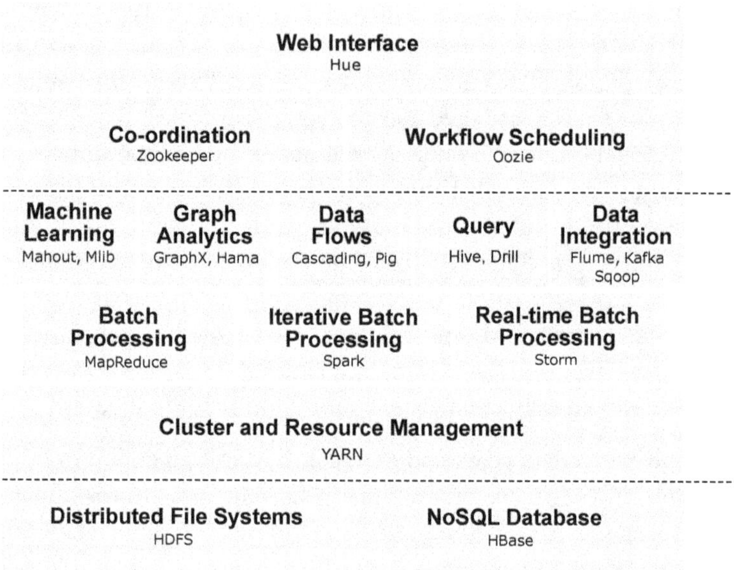

Figure 1.4. *Hadoop and its ecosystem (non-exhaustive)*

The Spark framework has been growing in reputation since 2014[3]. Originally developed in 2009 by AMPLab, from the University of California, Berkeley, the project became an Apache open source project in 2010. Spark, built on Hadoop and MapReduce, improves upon MapReduce by taking advantage of the nodes' random access memory when possible (via Resilient Distributed Datasets or RDD) and chaining together multiple processing steps

3 According to the Google Trends service, which statistically analyzes research subjects of interest to web users.

without systematically reading and writing to the hard disk as MapReduce does. This clever trick significantly speeds up the majority of data handling processes, such as sorting, word counting, unsupervised k-means classification or calculating PageRank centrality in a graph, by up to a factor of 5 [SHI 15]. Nevertheless, we note that according to [SHI 15], MapReduce performs better at managing the processes between the mapping and reducing phases. Furthermore, Spark comes with a complete environment, allowing (like MapReduce and Storm) real-time data flow problems as well as background (batch) tasks to be processed, for different types of data (text, graph, etc.). Applications can be written in Java, Scala or Python, and the MLib library (Spark Machine Learning Library), which comes from the data search library Mahout, from MapReduce, updates on the fly, all while offering an increasingly high-level data interface (RDDs have now been expanded into DataFrames, data displays that allow the data to be grouped in columns like in a table from a relational database).

Platforms specializing in decision-making solutions are also rapidly developing. They are offering more and more solutions for interfacing with open source tools. For example, SAS has offered SAS® Data Loader to interface with Hadoop, and since 2015 has clearly positioned itself with the main themes in the sector, such as cybersecurity or the Internet of Things. As another example, IBM is extending its IBM Cloud Bluemix platform with their Data Science Experience offering, based on Apache Spark. More specifically, this offering allows data scientists and developers access to 250 datasets, all powered by Spark and equipped with different open source software, like H2O, a Machine Learning solution. This data analysis software is not only compatible with big data platforms like Spark, but also claims to allow machine learning models developed in Python, Java or R to be easily deployed on these platforms. H2O is offered by a Californian start-up, H2O.ai.

According to KDnuggets [PIA 16], a site specializing in current affairs in business analytics, big data, data science and data mining, there are not many professionals who use only proprietary or indeed only open source solutions. A large majority of them use both families of tools. The dynamism of the open source community has made its technologies very popular to use. According to a 2013 survey run by O'Reilly, looking at data scientist salaries, the median salary of a data scientist who uses open source tools is 130,000 $US compared to 90,000 $US for those who only use proprietary tools.

According to the same site, the use of tools in the "Hadoop/Big data" category is becoming more accessible. Almost half of professionals use these tools (39% in 2016 compared to 29% in 2015 and 17% in 2014). This development is primarily due to the growth of Apache Spark, MLlib and H2O (see Table 1.2).

Tool	2016	2015	2015 –> 2016
Hadoop	22.1%	18.4%	+20.5%
Spark	21.6%	11.3%	+91%
Hive	12.4%	10.2%	+21.3%
MLlib	11.6%	3.3%	+253%
SQL on Hadoop tools	7.3%	7.2%	+1.6%
H2O	6.7%	2.0%	+234%
HBase	5.5%	4.6%	+18.6%
Apache Pig	4.6%	5.4%	–16.1%
Apache Mahout	2.6%	2.8%	–7.2%
Dato	2.4%	0.5%	+338%
Datameer	0.4%	0.9%	–52.3%
Other Hadoop/HDFS-based tools	4.9%	4.5%	+7.5%

Table 1.2. *Usage statistics for big data tools according to a survey of 2,895 respondents from the data analytics community and vendors. The respondents were from US/Canada (40%), Europe (39%), Asia (9.4%), Latin America (5.8%), Africa/Middle East (2.9%) and Australia/NZ (2.2%). They were asked about 102 different tools, including the "Hadoop/big data tools" shown here [PIA 16].*

Continuing to look at the data from KDnuggets [PIA 16], R appears to be the preferred tool of data scientists for data analytics. Usually used on an office machine with datasets of reasonable size, this language originally designed for statisticians is perfect for exploratory analysis, because it comes with libraries rich in algorithms for machine learning, evaluation, producing graphs, etc. Combined with offers such as H2O (or Rserver), it is now transferrable to the big data environment. However, Python, a computer programming language, is growing in popularity. Being flexible and open, and a generalist programming language, it is well suited to integrating analysis tasks with Web applications or with specific unconventional architectures. Its dedicated data science libraries make it a serious competitor to R.

1.4.2. *Migration towards a data-oriented strategy*

There are still very few companies who can boast of having migrated towards a data-oriented strategy. The specialist Internet press, informed by digital transformation consultants with a wide overview of these changes, agrees on four identifiable phases of big data adoption [DEM 16]:

1) experimentation with the big data platform;

2) implementation: developing first use cases;

3) expansion: deployment in multiple use cases;

4) optimization: integration with the business IT system.

The experimentation phase is when the potential of using a big data infrastructure is explored. The aim at this phase is to deal with installation and configuration. The main objective is to see how compatible the technology is with existing architecture. Such experimentation need not cost much because all that is required are a few bottom-of-the-range servers kitted out with open source software such as Hadoop/Spark. This experimentation phase very often results in the use of a data storage layer with pre-existing data, upon which a new layer of data handling is added, such as database queries.

Once the technical platform has been mastered, during the second implementation phase, the business tackles a use case that demonstrates the value of big data. This consists of developing a data processing chain for pre-existing data, then deploying this proof of concept in a production context. Common use cases at this stage include detecting fraud, log analysis for improved understanding of use patterns, predicting churn or, closer to the user experience, introducing recommendation systems. Data analytic libraries, such as MLib for Spark [SPA 16], have long lists of native (and optimized) algorithms for addressing these types of problems. The objective here is to demonstrate the value added and the economic impact of setting up a big data architecture.

The third phase is of course generalizing use cases to different levels of the business's value chain. The teams in charge of big data will by now have examples of early successes to help convince the different stakeholders in the business, and the cost of developing a new use case will be reduced since the infrastructure already exists. This is where business applications see the light of day, each service seizing upon technology to optimize existing analysis, extending it, proposing new analysis or simply gaining a better understanding of their field. A financial service will seek to improve risk management or fraud detection, a health service will launch targeted prevention programs, aim to reduce readmission or analyze internal processes to improve their coordination.

Finally, the last phase consists of true integration of data analytics and its insights into the overall strategy of the business. The improvement in business procedures and/or economic benefits is turned into competitive advantages. Results from predictive analysis inform decision-making. At this stage, the decision makers consult someone with responsibility for data (the job title Chief Data Officer is starting to appear) and a dedicated data team maintains the infrastructure and sets about solving new, ad-hoc problems specific to the business. The data analyst, a specialist in statistics, helps to produce dashboards displaying the data and to make best use of data processing chains, whereas the data scientist, with expertise in mathematics, statistics and computing, produces new data processing chains and unlocks new opportunities, while also making sure to maintain real-time visualization of the company's performance.

1.4.3. *Is migration towards a big data architecture necessary?*

Companies are inevitably considering whether or not to migrate towards a big data architecture. Does the existing business intelligence (BI) system need replacing? As a simplification, this type of system consists of two main parts:

– the ETL process (extracting, transforming and loading data), which consists of extracting from the company's operational data sources all the (heterogeneous) data that could help respond to the decision makers' questions. The data is then processed (cleaned, normalized, aggregated, etc.) and integrated so that it can be loaded into the data warehouse following predefined protocols;

– the data warehouse allowing all of a company's data to be consolidated and integrated and hence offering a cross-cutting and integrated overview of all aspects of the company's business. It can be made up of several subsets called datamarts which each characterize a defined business procedure. This data is structured in the form of multidimensional logical schemas allowing access to predefined indicators to be prepared, to fulfill a reporting requirement for example, while still allowing their analysis in several dimensions (for example, analyzing the "revenue" indicator "by region", "by period" or "by shop"). This modeling can be used to build multidimensional cubes (or hypercubes) on OLAP servers, allowing significant interactivity when searching. Graphical BI tools for analysis and reporting, like Excel, Table or Business Object, are often used to build dashboards and reports in consultation with the warehouse.

The arrival of big data has been accompanied by the emergence of new analytical processes (or workloads) that classical ETL or storage technologies would struggle to complete:

– exploratory analysis of raw, unmodeled and unstructured data;

– real-time processing, in contrast to ETL processes that run in batches;

– accelerated batch processing for large data volumes;

– agility and rapid data archiving, with the ability to rapidly repeat the processing necessary to update the warehouse data;

– complex analysis, such as the parallel application of many millions of scoring models on millions of bank accounts to detect fraud, for example.

The good news is that it is possible to bring the two worlds together and to use Hadoop as an efficient and scalable ETL solution for data that requires specific workloads. Once the data has been extracted and loaded in Hadoop, it can be subjected to complex transformations in batches by programming MapReduce or Spark jobs, or using high-level languages like HiveQL or Pig. It is possible to analyze (parse) the syntax of unstructured or semi-structured data, and to carry out calculations, joins and aggregations in order to integrate data from diverse sources, or to structure them so that they can be inserted into data warehouses following classical business workflows.

Hadoop can also be used to build a flexible and scalable data warehouse and to interface it with classical BI tools, for reporting for example. However, the majority of data warehousing solution publishers such as Oracle or Teradata prefer to integrate Hadoop at the ETL level only, which allows their solutions to be augmented rather than replaced. Conversely, proponents of open source solutions champion workload management in which the distributed Hadoop environment plays the role of a data hub through which all the data in the company ecosystem transits, before being fed into multiple analytical platforms.

Analyzing all of these approaches is complex. Some authors have produced grids comparing the requirements of different technical choices, such as the properties of the data analysis algorithms [LAN 15], as well as their potential implications, for example, regarding skills and human resources [CHA 13].

1.5. Challenges and opportunities for the world of insurance

Data lies at the heart of insurance. It is the raw material for scoring models, allowing segmentation of premium holders, to know them better and offer them bespoke products, to better estimate their current and future risk and to make decisions. Big data and the digital transition are hence profoundly changing the insurance sector. As for all economic actors, insurers will of course face changes of organization, culture and competition. We will illustrate this development with two examples in which big data plays a central role: the first illustrates the impact of the development of the sharing economy and the second the impact of changing behaviors on segmentation.

Insurance is already part of the sharing economy [LAC 15]. New actors, not necessarily from the world of insurance, are creating communities of individuals with specific insurance needs in order to negotiate highly personalized contracts for them from insurers, and reducing costs as they do so. If community platforms are allowing individuals to articulate their needs, big data is allowing these new actors to be proactive in finding small groups of clients whose frustration accumulates online. Indeed, all that is required is to analyze search engine enquiries, blogs and social networks to determine specific insurance needs. These new actors are thus changing the relationship between the insured and their insurers, but are also facilitating innovation since the (very) personalized solutions are either adaptations of existing contracts or completely new contracts. Although this type of market is still marginal, it seems likely for such a market of niches to be able to grow. This is particularly the case for the collaborative practices for sharing goods or services (carsharing, vehicle/apartment hire between individuals, etc.) which continue to develop. These are changing how risks are assessed and again specific, or even bespoke, warranties must be offered [INC 14]. Essentially, these practices are changing the paradigm from "one good for one owner" to "a multitude of users for one good". This shift from ownership towards usage is bringing about new types of risks and represents a challenge for insurers [LAC 15].

Big data also gives easy access to some of the information necessary for pricing and will gradually reduce the use of classical paper questionnaires. Hence, it allows faster decision-making. Even better, by giving access to previously inaccessible information, it will enable reduction in the existing information asymmetry [EWA 13] between the person being insured, who knows virtually all the information concerning them, and the insurer who has only partial information. Hence, big data allows greater knowledge of the insured and the risks associated with them, more precise evaluation of behavior and hence optimized selection of who to insure and fairer premium prices. Those being insured can, particularly if it is in their interest, give access to very private data about their way of life. The acceptability of such an approach, for consumers and regulators, is evidently critical [THO 15]. The slogan "pay as you live, drive etc." is already here, especially in automobile insurance. For example, connected driving allows precise analysis of driving style (speed, acceleration, braking, cornering, etc.), according to the road and weather conditions. This trend is also developing in health insurance with connected objects, allowing the physical condition (heart rate, sleep, etc.) and activity (number of steps taken, participation in sports, etc.) of the person being insured to be measured. The quality of their everyday environment can be evaluated using external and open data. However, "hyper-individualized" premium pricing could challenge the current model of segmentation and mutualization of risk [HOU 15], the underlying principle of how prices are set, and questions how risk portfolios will be structured [CHA 15]. The intrusion of insurers into the heart of individuals' private lives obviously poses the problem of data protection. There are also questions regarding how new practices will develop and how they might impact society.

Through these two examples, we have demonstrated some of the opportunities offered by big data (new markets, innovation and reduction in information asymmetry). Improving the effectiveness of advertising campaigns and of targeting and reducing fraud are further examples. New challenges are appearing (the entrance of intermediaries, the fundamentals of insurance under question, data security, actuarial challenges) while ethical, security and legal questions are also being raised. Regulators may restrict the use of personal data or data that leads to segmentation considered to be discriminatory. Markets for fraudulent profiles could develop, and alert premium holders will create different profiles for private and public use, thus challenging the benefit of the reduction in information asymmetry. Finally, if big data represents a profitable investment, it risks destabilizing the whole insurance market. On the one hand, companies without the means to access big data and the necessary technologies and workforce skills will see their competitivity unravel. They therefore risk disappearing or being bought out. On the other hand, intermediary platforms, notably GAFA (Google, Apple, Facebook, Amazon), who control the whole data value chain (collection, the technology for storage and calculations, relevant expertise), could seek to take a significant proportion of the profits, or could even be tempted to become insurers themselves. Buying out weakened companies could thus allow them to enter the insurance market. A new form of asymmetry, of control over data, is probably already in place.

1.6. Conclusion

Big data is here. Without doubt, the flood of data should continue, if not grow. If properly stored, managed and exploited, big data offers numerous opportunities. Computing has laid down a gauntlet: new architectures and a new ecosystem have been developed and are continually evolving. Insurance has not been spared from this phenomenon. Big data will allow new opportunities to be seized and also brings new risks. The final three chapters of this book will shed light on these developments.

However, big data cannot do everything, all the time. One famous example, among others, is the failure of Google's flu forecasting system (since abandoned) [LAZ 14]. Good predictions sometimes rely upon good understanding, and data science, despite inevitable changes to make and challenges to face, has bright days ahead of it. These issues as well as the main machine learning algorithms will be presented in the next two chapters.

1.7. Bibliography

[BOY 12] Boyd D., Crawford K., "Critical questions for big data: Provocations for a cultural, technological, and scholarly phenomenon", *Information, Communication & Society*, no. 5, pp. 662–679, 2012.

[CHA 13] Chalmers S., Bothorel C., Picot Clémente R., Big Data – State of the Art, Report, Télécom Bretagne, 2013.

[CHA 15] Charpentier A., Denuit M.M., Elie R., "Segmentation et mutualisation, les deux faces d'une même pièce?", *Risques*, no. 103, pp. 19–23, 2015.

[CHE 12] Chen H., Chiang R.H., Storey V.C., "Business intelligence and analytics: from big data to gig impact", *MIS Quarterly*, no. 4, pp. 1165–1188, 2012.

[CHE 14] Chen M., Mao S., Liu Y., "Big data: a survey", *Mobile Networks and Applications*, no. 2, pp. 171–209, 2014.

[DEL 14] Delforge P., "America's data centers consuming and wasting growing amounts of energy", *Natural Resource Defence Council*, 2014. Available at: https//:www.nrdc.org/resources/americas-data-centers-consuming-and-wasting-growing-amounts-energy, accessed 18th April 2017.

[DEM 16] Demarest G., "Four Phases of Operationalizing Big Data", *CIOReview*, 2016. Available at: http://bigdata.cioreview.com/cxoinsight/four-phases-of-operationalizing-big-data-nid-15251-cid-15.html, accessed 18th April 2017.

[DIE 12] Diebold F., On the Origin(s) and development of the term "Big Data", Pier Working Paper Archive, Penn Institute for Economic Research, 2012.

[EUD 16] Eudes Y., "Visite exceptionnelle dans le data center de Facebook, en Suède", *Le Monde*, 2016. Available at: http://www.lemonde.fr/ pixels/article/2016/06/03/les-datas-du-grand-froid_4932566_4408996.html, accessed 18th April 2017.

[EWA 13] Ewald F., Thourot P., "Big Data, défis et opportunités pour les assureurs", *ENASS Papers 5, Banque & Stratégie*, no. 315, pp. 5–8, 2013.

[FAN 13] Fan W., Bifet A., "Mining big data: current status, and forecast to the future", *ACM SIGKDD Explorations Newsletter*, no. 2, pp. 1–5, 2013.

[FAN 14] Fan J., Han F., Liu H., "Challenges of big data analysis", *National Science Review*, no. 2, pp. 293–314, 2014.

[GSM 15] GSMA, Unlocking the Value of IoT Through Big Data, Report, GSM Association, 2015.

[GU 14] Gu J., Zhang L., "Some comments on big data and data science", *Annals of Data Science*, nos 3–4, pp. 283–291, 2014.

[HAD 16] HADOOP, Welcome to Apache™ Hadoop®!, available at: http://hadoop.apache.org/, accessed 18th July 2016.

[HOU 15] Houlle O., "Le Big Data modifie le visage de l'assurance", *ENASS Papers 9, Banque & Stratégie*, no. 336, pp. 28–30, 2015.

[IBM 16] IBM, "IBM- What is big data?", 2016. Available at: https://www-01.ibm.com/software/data/bigdata/what-is-big-data.html, accessed 18th July 2016.

[INC 14] INC, "Consommation collaborative: quels enjeux et quelles limites pour les consommateurs?", *Colloque INC*, Ministère de l'Economie, de l'Industrie et du Numérique, Paris, France, 7th November 2014.

[KEL 15] Kelly J., Big Data Vendor Revenue and Market Forecast, 2011–2026, Report, WIKIBON, 2015.

[LAC 15] Lacaze O., "Le xxie siècle sera collaboratif, quid de l'assurance ?", *ENASS Papers 10, Banque & Stratégie*, no. 341, pp. 30–32, 2015.

[LAN 01] Laney D., "3D Data managment: controlling data volume, velocity and variety", *Application Delivery Strategies*, no. 949, 2001.

[LAN 15] Landset S., Khoshgoftaar T.M., Richter A.N. *et al.*, "A survey of open source tools for machine learning with big data in the Hadoop ecosystem", *Journal of Big Data*, no. 1, pp. 1–36, 2015.

[LAZ 14] Lazer D., Kennedy R., King G. *et al.*, "The Parable of Google Flu: Traps in Big Data Analysis", *Science*, no. 14, pp. 1203–1205, 2014.

[MAN 11] Manyika J., Chui M., Brown B. *et al.*, Big data: The next frontier for innovation, competition, and productivity, Report, The McKinsey Global Institute, 2011.

[PIA 16] Piatetsky G., "R, Python Duel As Top Analytics, Data Science software – KDnuggets 2016 Software Poll Results", KDNUGGETS, 2016, available at: http://www.kdnuggets.com/2016/06/r-python-top-analytics-data-mining-data-science-software.html, accessed 13th July 2016.

[SHI 15] Shi J., Qiu Y., Minhas U.F. *et al.*, "Clash of the titans: MapReduce vs. Spark for large scale data analytics", *Proceedings of the VLDB Endowment*, no. 13, pp. 2110–2121, 2015.

[SPA 16] Spark, Spark Machine Learning Library (MLlib) Guide, MLlib: Main Guide - Spark 2.1.0 Documentation, available at: http://spark.apache.org/docs/latest/mllib-guide.html, accessed 13th July 2016.

[STA 16a] StatisticBrain, Facebook Statistics, 2016, available at: http://www.statisticbrain.com/facebook-statistics/, accessed 13th July 2016.

[STA 16b] StatisticBrain, Google Annual Search Statistics, 2016, available at: http://www.statisticbrain.com/google-searches/, accessed 13th July 2016.

[THO 15] Thourot P., Nessi J.-M., Folly K.A., "Big data et tarification de l'assurance", *Risques*, no. 103, 2015.

[WAR 13] WARD J.S., BARKER A., "Undefined by data: a survey of big data definitions", *arXiv preprint arXiv:1309.5821*, 2013.

[WU 14] WU X., ZHU X., WU G.-Q. *et al.*, "Data mining with big data", *IEEE Transactions on Knowledge and Data Engineering*, no. 1, pp. 97–107, 2014.

[ZIK 11] ZIKOPOULOS P., EATON C., *Understanding Big Data: Analytics for Enterprise Class Hadoop and Streaming Data*, McGraw-Hill Osborne Media, New York, 2011.

2

From Conventional Data Analysis Methods to Big Data Analytics

2.1. From data analysis to data mining: exploring and predicting

Data analysis here mainly means descriptive and exploratory methods, also known as unsupervised. The objective is to describe as well as structure a set of data that can be represented in the form of a rectangular table crossing n statistical units and p variables. We generally consider n observations as points in p dimensional vector space, which, if provided with a distance, is a Euclidean space. Numerical variables are vectors of an n dimensional space. Data analysis methods are essentially dimension reduction methods that are divided into two categories:

– on the one hand, factor methods (principal component analysis for numeric variables, correspondence analyses for category variables) which lead to new numeric variables, combinations of the original variables, allowing representations in low dimensional spaces. Mathematically, these are variants of singular value decomposition of the data table;

– on the other hand, the unsupervised classification methods or clustering which divide observations, or variables, into homogeneous groups. The main algorithms are either hierarchical (step-by-step construction of the classes by successive clustering of units) or direct partition searches by k-means.

Many works are devoted to previous methods like [SAP 11].

Chapter written by Gilbert SAPORTA.

However, data analysis is also an attitude that consists of "letting the data speak" by putting nothing, or at least very little *a priori*, on the generating mechanism. Let us recall here the principle stated by [BEN 72]: "The model must follow the data, and not the opposite". Data analysis developed in the 1960s and 1970s in reaction to the abuses of formalization, see [ANS 67], regarding John Tukey: "He (Tukey) seems to identify statistics with the grotesque phenomenon generally known as mathematical statistics and find it necessary to replace statistics by data analysis."

Data mining, a movement which began in the 1990s at the intersection of statistics and information technologies (databases, artificial intelligence, machine learning, etc.), also aims at discovering structures in large datasets and promotes new tools, such as association rules. The metaphor of data mining means that there are treasures or nuggets hidden under mountains of data that can be discovered with specialized tools. Data mining is a step in the knowledge discovery process, which involves applying data analysis algorithms. [HAN 99] defined it thus: "I shall define data mining as the discovery of interesting, unexpected, or valuable structures in large data sets." Data mining analyzes data collected for other purposes: it is often a secondary analysis of databases, designed for the management of individual data, and where there is no concern about effectively collecting data (surveys, experimental designs).

Data mining also seeks to find predictive models of a Y denoted response, but from a very different perspective than that of conventional modeling. A model is nothing more than an algorithm and not a representation of the mechanism that generated the data. We then proceed by exploring a set of linear or nonlinear algorithms, explicit or not, in order to select the best, which is the one that provides the most accurate forecasts without falling into the overfitting trap. We distinguish regression methods where Y is quantitative, supervised classification methods (also called discrimination methods) where Y is categorical, most often with two modalities. Massive data processing has only reinforced the trends already present in data mining.

2.2. Obsolete approaches

Inferential statistics were developed in a context of scarce data, so much so that a sample of more than 30 units was considered large! The volume of data radically changes the practice of statistics. Here are some examples:

– any deviation from a theoretical value becomes "significant". Thus, a correlation coefficient of 0.01 calculated between two variables on a million observations (and even less, as the reader will easily verify) will be declared significantly different from zero. Is it a useful result?

– the confidence intervals of the parameters of a model become zero width since the latter is generally in $1/\sqrt{n}$. Does this mean that the model will be known with certainty?

In general, there is no longer a generative model that applies to a large amount of data no more than the rules of choice of model by penalized likelihood that are the subject of so many publications.

It should be noted that the criteria of the type:

$$AIC = -2ln(L) + 2k \qquad [2.1]$$

and $$BIC = -2ln(L) + ln(n)k \qquad [2.2]$$

to choose between simple models where k is the number of parameters and L the likelihood, become ineffective when comparing predictive algorithms where neither the likelihood nor the number of parameters are known, as in decision trees and more complex methods discussed in the next chapter. Note that it is illogical, as is often seen, to use *AIC* and *BIC* simultaneously since they come from two incompatible theories: Kullback–Leibler information for the first and Bayesian choice of models *a priori* equiprobable for the second.

The large volume of data could be an argument in favor of the asymptotic properties of *BIC*, if it were calculable, since it has been shown that the probability of choosing the true model tends to 1 when the number of observations tends to infinity. The true model, however, must be part of the family studied, and it is especially necessary that this "true" model exists, which is fiction: a model (in the generative sense) is only a simplified representation of reality. Thirty years ago, well before we talked about big data, George Box declared "All models are wrong, some are useful."

The abuses of the so-called conventional statistics had been vigorously denounced by John Nelder [NEL 85], the co-inventor of generalized linear models, in this 1985 text discussing Chatfield's article: "Statistics is intimately connected with science and technology, and few mathematicians have experience or understand the methods of either. This I believe is what lies behind the grotesque emphasis on significance tests in statistics courses of all kinds; a mathematical apparatus has been erected with the notions of power, uniformly most powerful tests, uniformly most powerful unbiased tests, etc. etc. and this is taught to people, who, if they come away with no other notion, will remember that statistics is about significant differences [...]. The apparatus on which their statistics course has been constructed is often worse than irrelevant, it is misleading about what is important in examining data and making inferences."

2.3. Understanding or predicting?

The use of learning algorithms leads to methods known as "black boxes" that empirically show that it is not necessary to understand in order to predict. This fact, which is disturbing for scientists, is explicitly claimed by learning theorists, such as [VAP 06] who writes "Better models are sometimes obtained by deliberately avoiding to reproduce the true mechanisms."

[BRE 01] confirmed this in his famous article of Statistical Science entitled "Statistical Modeling: The Two Cultures": "Modern statistical thinking makes a clear distinction between the statistical model and the world. The actual mechanisms underlying the data are considered unknown. The statistical models do not need to reproduce these mechanisms to emulate the observable data." Breiman thus contrasted two modeling cultures in order to draw conclusions from data: one assumes that data is generated by a given stochastic model, and the other considers the generating mechanism as unknown and uses algorithms.

In the first case, attention is paid to fitting the model to the data (goodness of fit) and in the second, focus is on forecast accuracy.

[DON 15] recently took up this discussion by talking of generative modeling culture and predictive modeling culture. The distinction between models for understanding and models for predicting was also explicit in [SAP 08] and [SHM 10].

2.4. Validation of predictive models

The quality of a forecasting model cannot be judged solely by the fact that it appropriately fits to the data: it has to provide good forecasts in the future, what is called the capacity of generalization. Indeed, it is easy to see that the more complex a model, for example a higher degree polynomial, the better it will fit to the data until it passes through all points, but this apparent quality will degrade for new observations: this is the overfitting phenomenon.

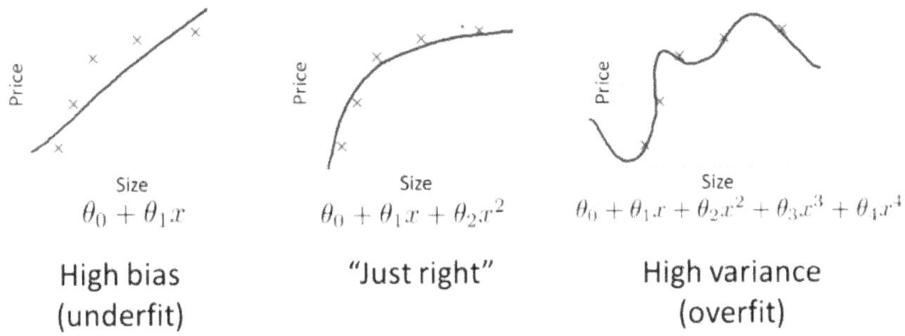

Figure 2.1. *From underfitting to overfitting (source: available at http://datascience.stackexchange.com/questions/361/when-is-a-model-underfitted)*

It is therefore appropriate to seek models that behave in a comparable way on available data (or learning data) and on future data. But this is not a sufficient criterion, since, for example, the constant model $\hat{y} = c$ verifies this property! Forecasts must also be of good quality.

2.4.1. *Elements of learning theory*

The inequalities of the learning statistical theory make it possible to find bounds for the difference between learning error and generalization error (future data) according to the number of observations in learning and the complexity of the family of models. Let us illustrate one of these inequalities in the case of supervised classification in two classes. A classifier is then a function of $f(x)$ predictors such that if $f(x) > 0$ we classify x observation in one group, and if $f(x) < 0$ in the other group. Points such as $f(x) = 0$ define the boundary.

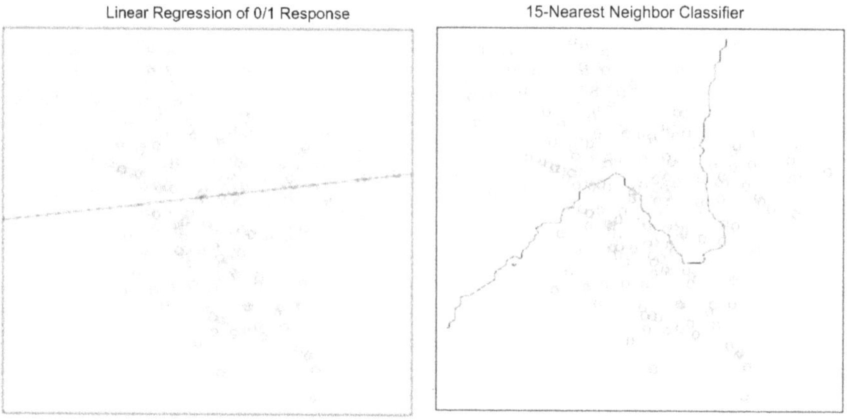

Figure 2.2. *A linear and nonlinear classifier (according to [HAS 09]). For a color version of the figure, see www.iste.co.uk/corlosquet-habart/insurance.zip*

The classifier error rate, which is a random variable because it depends on the sample, is the proportion of wrongly classified observations. Its expectation is called empirical risk, and denoted as R_{emp}. For future observations coming from the same unknown distribution, it will be denoted as R. Let us consider families of classifiers, such as fixed degree d polynomial functions, with or without constraints on the coefficients, or that of the k-nearest neighbors (we allocate to the majority class among the k neighbors of a "member"). The learning theory has shown that the complexity of these models does not depend on the number of parameters, but on the ability to separate points by the boundary $f(x)$: it is VC dimension or Vapnik–Chervonenkis dimension, denoted as h thereafter. For example, the linear boundaries of $\mathbb{R}^p$ allow us to separate $p + 1$ points belonging to different groups but not $p + 2$ points: more precisely, there are always configurations of $p + 2$ non-separable points, even if there are sometimes configurations of $p + 1$ non-separable points. VC dimension is $h = p + 1$.

One of the most famous inequalities states that, with a probability $1 - \alpha$:

$$R < R_{\text{emp}} + \sqrt{\frac{h\left(\ln(2n/h)+1\right)-\ln(\alpha/4)}{n}} \qquad [2.3]$$

For fixed n, the increase of h leads R_{emp} to 0 (overfitting) but the radical increases thus the existence of an optimal complexity h*.

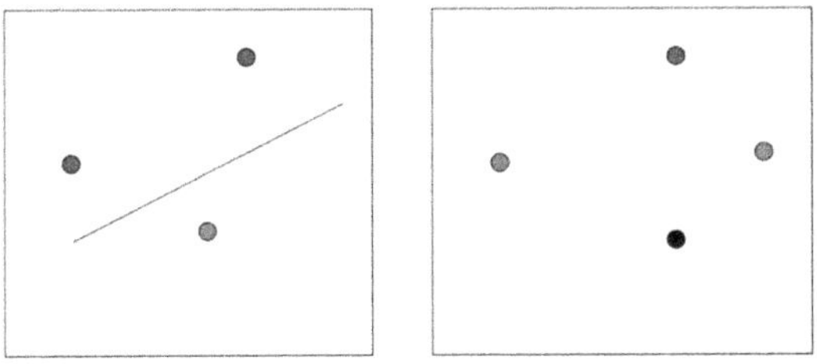

Figure 2.3. *In a plane, some configurations of four points are not linearly separable*

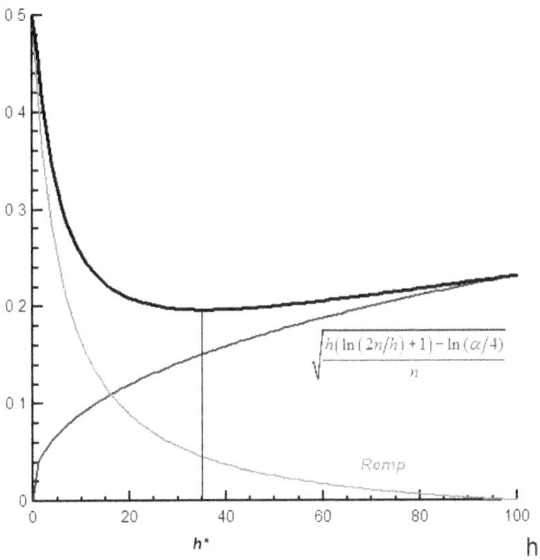

Figure 2.4. *Optimal VC dimension. For a color version of the figure, see www.iste.co.uk/corlosquet-habart/insurance.zip*

It should be noted that the gap between empirical risk and risk depends only on the ratio n/h and that if n is increased faster than h, there is convergence. This result shows that the more data we have, the more complex models we can use.

The statistical learning theory abounds with such inequalities, but unfortunately they are not very convenient in practice to choose a model because VC dimension is difficult to obtain. Cross-validation methods are therefore indispensable: they consist of setting aside one or more parts of the data in order to simulate the behavior of algorithms or models in the presence of future data.

We must strongly reiterate that the validation of a model or algorithm in big data can only be carried out on "new" data, which make it possible to ensure the reproducibility of results. This is an essential difference from standard statistical practice, although some so-called leave-one-out methods have been used for a long time in discrimination. Nevertheless, removing an observation when n is large is of little effect.

2.4.2. *Cross-validation*

To choose between several models or algorithms, the practice involves randomly dividing the available data into three subsets including learning, validation and test. Typical values for the proportions of these three subsets are 50%, 25% and 25% [HAS 09]. The learning set is used to estimate the parameters of (or to calibrate) each model. Each of the models is then applied to the validation set to select the best according to the criterion chosen (R^2, misclassification rate, etc.). The best model is then applied to the test set to estimate its performance, which is overvalued in the previous phase since one takes the *sup* of a set. We thus distinguish the evaluation of the performance of a model, from the choice of this model. Once the model is chosen, it must be re-estimated using all available data before putting it into production.

Ideally, in order to avoid risks due to random splitting in learning, validation and test, it would be necessary to iterate this step, but this is not done for very large datasets. For small size sets, it will be preferable to subdivide the set into 5 or 10 parts of equal number: in a rotating manner, a model is estimated by removing one of the 5 or 10 parts (5- or 10-fold cross-validation) and evaluating its performance on the part set side and then averaging the results.

2.5. Combination of models

Rather than choosing the best among M models or algorithms, it is usually much more efficient to combine them. We then talk of ensemble methods; boosting, bagging, random forests fall into this category, but only combine classifiers or regressors of the same family as trees. The same is true of Bayesian model averaging, which linearly combines submodels of the same family, with the posterior probabilities of each model knowing the data as coefficients. While remaining faithful to data analysis principles, we will not discuss Bayesian model averaging which involves constraining hypotheses in order to be applied.

A particularly well-suited method for massive data is stacking, which has yielded excellent results in machine learning competitions, the most famous of which is the million-dollar Netflix prize. In 2009, the two best solutions combined numerous models according to the stacking technique introduced by [WOL 92] and [BRE 96]. Let us start with the context of regression. Let us consider M predictions: $\hat{y}_m = f_m(\mathrm{x}) \quad m = 1, \ldots, M$ obtained using M models or different algorithms, which could be of any type: linear or nonlinear, neural networks, regression trees, etc. The very simple idea is to look for a linear combination: $\hat{y} = \sum_{m-1}^{M} w_m f_m(x)$, which provides a sum of squared minimum errors. In the original version, to avoid that the more complex models have more weight because they predict better in learning, the criterion is modified so that the predictions of each y_i are done by removing observation i (predicted residuals):

$$\min \sum_{i=1}^{n} \left(y_i - \sum_{m=1}^{M} w_m f_m^{-1}(x_i) \right)^2 \qquad [2.4]$$

but when n is large, it has little impact.

On the contrary, as shown by [NOC 16], the estimation of weights w_i is made unstable by the fact that the predictions of the different models are highly correlated with one another as soon as these models are efficient. It is therefore necessary to regularize the least squares. One possibility is to carry out a regression of y on m predictions without constant term, under the constraint that weights w_i are positive and of sum equal to 1, as in Bayesian model averaging. A simpler solution is to carry out a PLS regression (see section 2.6.1.2): as the M predictions are positively correlated, a single PLS component is generally sufficient, and ensures the positivity of weights.

Extension to supervised classification is carried out while taking for $\hat{y}_m$ value the probability of belonging to the class of interest. Since the y_i are binary, we will use a PLS logistic regression instead of a PLS regression to estimate the weights.

Extensions of predictors to geometric means have been proposed, as well as the search for areas of competence of each predictor or combinations of some of them. However, in practice, stacking proves to be very effective because, by construction, the optimal linear combination of M predictions is necessarily better than each of them.

2.6. The high dimension case

The data may also be massive in the sense that p, the number of variables, is much greater than n, the number of observations. This is the case for data from the Web or biology, where it is not uncommon to count several thousands of variables. Predictive methods of regression type cannot be applied when $p>>n$, since the least square estimator does not exist. If we want to preserve all the predictors, we will resort to regularization methods, or otherwise to sparse methods.

2.6.1. *Regularized regressions*

They proceed either by projection onto subspaces or by constraining the coefficient vector. The estimators are biased and properties invariant under change of scale are lost. The data will be centered and reduced prior to the application of methods.

2.6.1.1. *Principal component regression*

This is undoubtedly the oldest method, applied in econometrics by Edmond Malinvaud in 1964 to solve multicollinearity problems. It involves reducing the space of the predictors by using $q < p$ principal components and then regressing Y response on these components by ordinary least squares. The principal components being linear combinations of predictors, we ultimately obtain a combination of predictors:

$$\hat{\mathbf{y}} = \mathbf{C}\hat{\alpha} = \alpha_1\mathbf{c}_1 + \ldots + \alpha_q\mathbf{c}_q = \mathbf{X}\hat{\boldsymbol{\beta}} \qquad [2.5]$$

Coefficient $\hat{\boldsymbol{\alpha}}$ and $\hat{\boldsymbol{\beta}}$ vectors are obtained simply by using the reconstruction formula q (truncated SVD) $\mathbf{X} = \mathbf{CU}'$ where $\mathbf{C}$ is the principal component matrix and $\mathbf{U}$ is the principal factor orthogonal matrix:

$$\hat{\boldsymbol{\beta}} = (\mathbf{X'X})^{+}\mathbf{X'Y} = (\mathbf{UC'CU'})^{+}\mathbf{UC'y} = \left(\mathbf{U}\frac{\mathbf{1}}{\mathbf{n}}\mathbf{C'CU'}\right)^{+}\frac{\mathbf{1}}{\mathbf{n}}\mathbf{UC'y}$$
$$= (\mathbf{U\Lambda U'})^{+}\frac{\mathbf{1}}{\mathbf{n}}\mathbf{UC'y} = \mathbf{U\Lambda^{+}U'U}\frac{\mathbf{1}}{\mathbf{n}}\mathbf{C'y} = \mathbf{U\Lambda^{+}}\frac{\mathbf{1}}{\mathbf{n}}\mathbf{C'y} = \mathbf{U}\hat{\boldsymbol{\alpha}} \qquad [2.6]$$

The symbol + refers to the Moore–Penrose inverse.

Here

$$\hat{\boldsymbol{\beta}} = \mathbf{U}\,\hat{\boldsymbol{\alpha}} \qquad \hat{\boldsymbol{\alpha}} = \mathbf{U}'\hat{\boldsymbol{\beta}} \qquad [2.7]$$

and

$$V(\hat{\beta}_j) = \sigma^2 \sum_{k=1}^{q} \frac{u_{jk}^2}{\lambda_k} \qquad [2.8]$$

In general, q is selected by cross-validation, but the regression on principal components has the following drawback: the principal components depend only on the predictors and not on the response, and their ranking does not necessarily reflect the correlations with this response.

2.6.1.2. *PLS regression*

Developed by H. and S. Wold, PLS regression resembles principal component regression, since data are also projected onto linear uncorrelated combinations of predictors. The main difference is that the PLS components are optimized to also be predictive of Y, whereas the principal components only extract the maximum variance of predictors without taking Y into account. The criterion used to obtain the first PLS component $\mathbf{t} = \mathbf{Xw}$ is Tucker's criterion:

$$\max_{\mathrm{w}} \operatorname{cov}^2(\mathrm{y}, \mathbf{Xw}) \qquad [2.9]$$

As

$$\operatorname{cov}^2(\mathrm{y}, \mathbf{Xw}) = r^2(\mathrm{y}, \mathbf{Xw})\, V(\mathrm{y})\, V(\mathbf{Xw}) \qquad [2.10]$$

we have a compromise between maximizing the correlation between **t** and y (regression) and maximizing the variance of **t** (PCA of predictors).

The solution is as follows: for the first PLS component, the w_j coefficient of each variable is, up to a multiplicative constant, equal to the covariance between $\mathbf{x}_j$ and $\mathbf{y}$, which ensures the consistency of signs. The following components are obtained by deflation, that is, by iterating the process on the residuals of Y and predictors after regression on $\mathbf{t}$. The simplicity of the algorithm, which requires neither diagonalization nor matrix inversion, makes it possible to process massive data. We will refer to [TEN 98] for more details.

2.6.1.3. *Ridge regression*

Invented by Hoerl and Kennard in the 1970s, this is a particular case of Tikhonov regularization: to avoid unstable coefficients, we add a constraint on their norm:

$$\min \|\mathrm{y} - \mathbf{X}\boldsymbol{\beta}\|^2 \text{ under } \|\boldsymbol{\beta}\|^2 \leq c^2 \qquad [2.11]$$

This is equivalent to adding a constant to the diagonal elements of **X'X** to "facilitate" the inversion:

$$\hat{\boldsymbol{\beta}}_R = \left(\mathbf{X}'\mathbf{X} + k\mathbf{I}\right)^{-1} \mathbf{X}'\mathbf{y} \qquad [2.12]$$

The constant k is determined by cross-validation.

2.6.2. *Sparse methods*

The preceding methods make it possible to obtain a function of all the variables, which becomes a disadvantage when p is very large: how can a linear combination of several hundreds or several thousands of variables be interpreted? Rather than resorting to stepwise selection techniques, the use of constraints in L_1 norm effectively solves the problem by enabling both selection and regularization.

2.6.2.1. *The Lasso*

Lasso or least absolute shrinkage and selection operator introduced in [TIB 96] consists of minimizing the residual sum of squares, with a bound on the sum of the absolute values of regression coefficients (L_1 penalty):

$$\min \|\mathbf{y} - \mathbf{X}\boldsymbol{\beta}\|^2 \text{ with } \sum_{j=1}^{p} |\beta_j| < c \qquad [2.13]$$

which is equivalent to:

$$\min\left(\|\mathbf{y}-\mathbf{X}\boldsymbol{\beta}\|^2+\lambda\sum_{j=1}^{p}|\beta_j|\right) \quad [2.14]$$

When c decreases, the regression coefficients reduce and some are canceled due to the use of the L_1 norm. The parameter c is generally obtained by cross-validation, with the aim of having the best predictor of Y.

Many developments followed: sparse variants of PLS regression, and also the group Lasso which applies in the case where the predictors are divided into blocks: the method then helps to eliminate entire blocks of variables.

2.6.2.2. *Sparse principal component analysis (PCA) and multiple correspondence analysis (MCA)*

In the same vein, sparse versions of principal component analysis have been proposed since the 2000s. There are several versions, but the most widely used is inspired by the Lasso and ridge regression, noting that the SVD can be interpreted as a ridge regression of components on the variables because the main factors are bounded. We obtain "components" that are combinations of a small number of initial variables, which facilitate interpretation, but at the expense of the loss of orthogonality properties of the components and/or factors.

[BER 12] developed a sparse version of multiple correspondence analysis as follows: the MCA being a PCA of blocks of indicators, the authors adapted the group Lasso to sparse PCA defined previously.

2.7. The end of science?

Big data processing requires new tools (we have briefly presented some), and a new attitude towards models that are just algorithms, based on validation with data set aside.

These new tools can be useful to specialists in a field, as [VAR 14] advises econometricians.

In a provocative article, [AND 08] claimed that the data deluge renders the scientific approach obsolete and declared in essence that: "correlations are enough, we can stop modeling. Let us load the data in larger computers and allow statistical algorithms to find structures where science cannot."

It is clear that correlation is not causality: a model that accurately predicts statistically does not necessarily allow for action. It is too often believed that the influence of a variable can be measured by its coefficient in the simple case of a linear model, or by elimination in complex cases: as in sensitivity analysis, we study the variation of a quality criterion (R^2, % of accurately classified observations, etc.) by removing the variable considered. This may be interesting but is still insufficient: on the one hand, to vary a variable "all things being equal" is an illusion, for the modification of a variable can entail modifications on those that are correlated to it, and thus on the response. On the other hand, without a pattern of causality, we cannot know how the other variables react in view of an intervention.

If we can often forecast without understanding, can we not better forecast if we do understand? This subject has been discussed in numerous meetings and studies by learning and causality specialists who introduce experimentation in big data (see [BOT 13]).

2.8. Bibliography

[AND 08] ANDERSON C., "The end of theory: the data deluge makes the scientific method obsolete", *Wired Magazine*, available at: https://www.wired.com/2008/06/pb-theory/, (last visited on April 15, 2017), 2008.

[ANS 67] ANSCOMBE F.J., "Topics in the investigation of linear relations", *Journal of the Royal Statistical Society*, vol. B 29, pp. 1–52, 1967.

[BEN 72] BENZÉCRI J.P., *L'Analyse des Données, Tome 2*, Dunod, Paris, 1972.

[BER 12] BERNARD A., GUINOT C., SAPORTA G., "Sparse principal component analysis for multiblock data and its extension to sparse multiple correspondence analysis", in COLUBI A. (ed.), *Compstat Proceedings*, 2012.

[BOT 13] BOTTOU L. *et al.*, "Counterfactual reasoning and learning systems: the example of computational advertising", *Journal of Machine Learning Research*, no. 14, pp. 3207–3260, 2013.

[BRE 96] BREIMAN L., "Stacked regressions", *Machine Learning*, no. 24, pp. 49–64, 1996.

[BRE 01] BREIMAN L., "Statistical modeling: The two cultures", *Statistical Science*, vol. 16, no. 3, pp. 199–215, 2001.

[DON 15] DONOHO D., 50 years of Data Science, Tukey Centennial workshop, available at: http://courses.csail.mit.edu/18.337/2015/docs/50YearsDataScience.pdf, (consulted April 15, 2017), 2015.

[HAN 99] HAND D., "Why data mining is more than statistics write large", *ISI*, Helsinki, available at: http://www.stat.fi/isi99/proceedings/arkisto/varasto/hand0490.pdf, (consulted April 15, 2017), 1999.

[HAS 09] HASTIE T., TIBSHIRANI R., FRIEDMAN J., *The Elements of Statistical Learning*, 2nd edition, Springer, New York, 2009.

[NEL 85] NELDER J.A., Discussion of CHATFIELD C., "The initial examination of data", *Journal of the Royal Statistical Society*, Series A, no. 148, pp. 214–253, 1985.

[NOC 16] NOÇAIRI H., GOMES C., THOMAS M. *et al.*, "Improving stacking methodology for combining classifiers; applications to cosmetic industry", *Electronic Journal of Applied Statistical Analysis*, vol. 9, no. 2, pp. 340–361, 2016.

[SAP 08] SAPORTA G., "Models for understanding versus models for prediction", in BRITO I. (ed.), *Compstat Proceedings*, Physica Verlag, 2008.

[SAP 11] SAPORTA G., *Probabilités, Analyse des données et statistique,* 3rd edition, Technip, Paris, 2011.

[SHM 10] SHMUELI G., "To explain or to predict?", *Statistical Science*, no. 25, pp. 289–310, 2010.

[TEN 98] TENENHAUS M., *La régression PLS*, Technip, Paris, 1998.

[TIB 96] TIBSHIRANI R., "Regression shrinkage and selection via the Lasso", *Journal of the Royal Statistical Society*, Series B, no. 58, pp. 267–288, 1996.

[VAP 06] VAPNIK V., *Estimation of Dependences Based on Empirical Data*, 2nd edition, Springer, New York, 2006.

[VAR 14] VARIAN H., "Big Data: New Tricks for Econometrics", *Journal of Economic Perspectives*, no. 28, pp. 3–28, 2014.

[WOL 92] WOLPERT D., "Stacked generalization", *Neural Networks*, no. 5, pp. 241–259, 1992.

3

Statistical Learning Methods

3.1. Introduction

The objective of this chapter is to present the statistical learning methods most commonly used in actuarial science. These are complementary methods to the more conventional statistical models, such as linear and logistic regression, which have long been applied in actuarial science. With the massive influx of digital data, it becomes convenient to implement more sophisticated data-processing and prediction methods. Examples of possible applications include:

– estimation of the amounts and frequencies of individual property claims and casualty insurance;

– estimation of individual medical expenses in health insurance;

– detection of fraud upon declaration of property and claims insurance;

– detection of borrowers at risk of default;

– development of insurance zones taking into account geographical information, such as open data;

– taking into account data collected in real time on vehicles for the purpose of establishing a more targeted car insurance rate (pay-how-you-drive concept).

Before presenting different learning methods more precisely, a general distinction should be made between supervised and unsupervised methods.

Chapter written by Franck VERMET.

3.1.1. *Supervised learning*

In this case, the presence of a Y variable to be explained is fundamental: having jointly observed the Y variable and explanatory variables on a sample of individuals, the objective is to construct a model that will allow the output Y associated with a new input to be predicted. The mathematical framework of supervised statistical learning is this. We define a learning sample: $L_n = \{(X_1, Y_1), \dots, (X_n, Y_n)\}\}$, that is, a sequence of independent and identically distributed random vectors (i.i.d.), having the same law as a random vector (X, Y). The law of the (X, Y) couple is unknown, and the objective of supervised statistical learning is to learn it by observing the learning base L_n. The random variables or X and Y vectors do not play the same role: in practice, X refers to the input variable (usually a vector consisting of explanatory variables) and Y refers to the output variable (also called the variable to be explained). The Y variable can also be multidimensional. The purpose of supervised learning is to learn the link between the X and Y variables: note that the knowledge of the marginal laws of X and Y is not sufficient to know the law of the (X, Y) couple. It is by a statistical approach based on the observation of L_n that we will obtain information, making it possible to predict a value $\hat{y}$ associated with a new observation of the input variable x, for which the y variable to be explained is unknown. Depending on the nature of the output variable y, we can distinguish two supervised statistical learning frameworks: regression and classification.

In the case of regression, the output variable Y is a quantitative variable, with real values. The standard framework is then:

$$\mathrm{Y} = \mathrm{f(X)} + \varepsilon, \qquad [3.1]$$

where f is the unknown function, called the regression function that we seek to estimate. The variable ε is a zero-expectation real random variable: it represents the noise and makes it possible to take into account the fact that the Y variable is only partially explained by the X variable. The learning base is then made up of couples: $(X_i, Y_i = \mathrm{f}(Xi) + \varepsilon_i)$, where ε_i are independent random variables and of the same law.

We also assume that the noise variable ε is conditionally centered on X. We then have: $\mathbb{E}[Y \mid X] = f(X)$, which defines the function f in a unique manner. Without any additional constraint on the function f, we can consider a nonparametric regression model, which therefore consists of constructing a predictor $\hat{f}$ from the learning base L_n, making it possible to better predict the output y associated with an input x. The quality of $\hat{f}$ can be measured, for example, by the mean squared error of generalization defined by: $E[(\hat{f}(X)-Y)^2]$. Since the law of the (X, Y) couple is unknown, in practice, the performance of the predictor is rather measured by an empirical mean squared error:

$$R_m(\hat{f}, \tilde{L}_m) = \frac{1}{m}\sum_{i=1}^{m}(\tilde{Y}_i - \hat{f}(\tilde{X}_i))^2, \quad [3.2]$$

defined on a test sample: $\tilde{L}_m = \{(\tilde{X}_1, \tilde{Y}_1), \dots, (\tilde{X}_m, \tilde{Y}_m)\}$ of size m, independent of L_n, where $(\tilde{X}_i, \tilde{Y}_i)$ are of the same law as (X, Y).

To practically implement a supervised learning method, it is necessary to restrict the class of regression functions considered, and the techniques for determining a predictor will then depend on this choice. A conventional option that we will not discuss here is linear regression, where $f(X)$ is assumed to be a linear combination of explanatory variables. In this case, the minimization of the empirical mean squared error calculated on the learning set leads to the resolution of a system of linear equations, which provides an explicit solution. For more sophisticated models, mostly nonlinear, the choice and the search for the "best" model are no longer quite simple as we will see in the subsequent sections.

In the case of classification, the output variable Y is discrete and represents the class to which the observation belongs. If K denotes the number of classes, we can consider that Y has values in $\{1, \dots, K\}$. The objective is to construct a model which associates to each input vector X a class in $\{1, \dots, K\}$. A common approach is to proceed in two steps: the model actually estimates the quantities: $P[Y = k \mid X = x]$, for $k \in \{1, \dots, K\}$, from which the class associated with the observation x is chosen.

We will present the following supervised learning methods in the subsequent sections: decision trees, layered neural networks, SVM (support vector machines) and model aggregation methods (bagging, random forests, boosting, stacking).

3.1.2. *Unsupervised learning*

In this case, there is no variable to be explained, which therefore rather concerns a clustering problem. The objective is to construct homogeneous classes that group together the most similar individuals (relative to the variables describing them), and the classes have to be as dissimilar as possible. The goal is to organize the information contained in the data, in order to make it more visible and better exploitable. Among the conventional methods, we have the ascending hierarchical classification and algorithms by dynamic reallocation (k-means). In section 3.6, we will see the Kohonen self-organizing map method, which has the advantage of allowing a graphical representation of the classes in a small space.

3.2. Decision trees

The principle of decision trees is to partition the space of the values of the explanatory variables into rectangles, on which the variable to be explained is constant. This very simple idea, which was developed by Breiman *et al.* [BRE 84] under the acronym CART (classification and regression tree), makes it possible to obtain an easy-to-visualize and simple-to-interpret model, which thus constitutes a genuine tool for supporting decision-making. Moreover, this method, which consists of recursively partitioning the input space in a dyadic way, can be applied in regression as well as in classification.

Let us describe the method in the case of the following model: (X, Y) is a random vector with values in $R^p \times G$, where $\mathcal{G} = \mathbb{R}$ in the case of regression and $G = \{1, \dots, K\}$ in the case of classification. We assume we know a learning set: $L_n = \{(x_i, y_i) \in R^p \times G, i = 1, \dots, n\}$, where (x_i, y_i) are independent realizations of random variables with the same law as (X, Y). At each stage of the partitioning, part of the input space is split into two sub-parts and a binary tree is naturally associated with the constructed partition:

– the root n_1 of the tree is associated with the entire input space and thus contains all the observations of L_n;

– the first step of the CART involves dividing this space into two, by choosing a split of the form: $\{X^j \leq s\} \cup \{X^j > s\}$, where $j \in \{1, \dots, p\}$, $X = (X^1, \dots, X^p)$ and $s \in \mathbb{R}$. Splitting thus means that all the observations having a value of the *j*th variable smaller than *s* are assigned to the left sub-tree and the others to the right sub-tree. For this to be relevant, the method selects the best possible (j, s) split, minimizing a $\mathcal{C}(j, s)$ cost function. Note: $x_i = (x_i^1, \dots, x_i^p)$,

$$n_{1,-}(j, s) = \{i \in \{1, \dots, n\}: x_i^j \leq s\} \quad [3.3]$$

and:

$$n_{1,+}(j, s) = \{i \in \{1, \dots, n\}: x_i^j > s\}. \quad [3.4]$$

In the case of regression, the function to be minimized is:

$$\mathcal{C}(s, j) = \sum_{i \in n_{1,-}(j,s)} (y_i - \overline{y_-})^2 + \sum_{i \in n_{1,+}(j,s)} (y_i - \overline{y_+})^2 \quad [3.5]$$

where:

$$\overline{y_-} = \frac{1}{card(n_{1,-}(j,s))} \sum_{i \in n_{1,-}(j,s)} y_i \quad [3.6]$$

and:

$$\overline{y_+} = \frac{1}{card(n_{1,+}(j,s))} \sum_{i \in n_{1,+}(j,s)} y_i. \quad [3.7]$$

We therefore seek to minimize the variance of the two sub-trees obtained. In the case of classification, the function to be minimized is:

$$\mathcal{C}(s, j) = \sum_{k=1}^{K} \hat{p}_{n_{1,-}(j,s)}^k \left(1 - \hat{p}_{n_{1,-}(j,s)}^k\right) + \sum_{k=1}^{K} \hat{p}_{n_{1,+}(j,s)}^k \left(1 - \hat{p}_{n_{1,+}(j,s)}^k\right), \quad [3.8]$$

where $\hat{p}_{n_{1,\pm}(j,s)}^k$ is the proportion of observations of the class k in the set $n_{1,\pm}(j, s)$. In this case, we try to minimize the Gini index of each set and thus to obtain the most homogeneous sub-trees possible (a set is perfectly homogeneous if all the observations are in the same class).

Once the root of the tree is partitioned, the process is iterated on each of the two sub-trees obtained, again searching for the optimal split for the chosen cost function, and so on until the stopping criterion is achieved. A classic stopping criterion involves not splitting a node of the tree that contains less than a fixed number of observations. The terminal nodes, which are no longer split, are called the leaves of the tree. Note that a pure node, that is, a node containing only observations with the same output value, is not split. The T_{max} tree obtained by this procedure is called the maximal tree, and for an observation belonging to a leaf n, this model predicts as the regression output value the mean value: $\overline{y_n} = \frac{1}{\mathrm{card(n)}} \sum_{i \in n} y_i$ (and the majority class of the observations of L_n present in the leaf, in classification).

The second step of the CART algorithm consists of a pruning step, which will select the best-pruned tree from the maximal tree T_{max} (in the sense of generalization error). This step is necessary because T_{max}, due to its very fine construction, is of low bias, but can be of very great variance: it is very dependent on the observations used but is also subject to overlearning. It is therefore necessary to select a model that may be somewhat less precise but capable of providing predictions of equivalent quality for new observations. In contrast to the maximal tree, the tree consisting only of its root has a zero variance, but a significant bias. The objective is therefore to find an intermediate tree between these two extremes. To do this, we start by constructing a sequence $(T_j)_{1 \le j \le J}$ of sub-trees pruned from each other, from T_{max}, corresponding to a family of nested partitions. Let us describe the procedure in the case of regression: We obtain this sequence $(T_j)_{1 \le j \le J}$ by minimizing a penalized criterion defined for every pruned sub-tree T of T_{max} and for all $\alpha \ge 0$ by:

$$Crit_\alpha(T) = \frac{1}{n} \sum_{i=1}^{n} (y_i - \hat{y}_{T,i})^2 + \alpha\, |T|, \qquad [3.9]$$

where $|T|$ is the number of leaves of T and $\hat{y}_{T,i}$ is the value predicted by the model associated with T for input x_i. By gradually increasing α, the minimization of $Crit_\alpha$ provides a sequence $(T_j)_{1 \le j \le J}$ with fewer and fewer leaves. It then remains to select a candidate in the sequence thus obtained. Breiman *et al.* proposed essentially two methods: using a test sample or proceeding by cross-validation. The first method assumes that there is an available test base: $\tilde{L}_{n_t} = \{(\tilde{x}_i, \tilde{y}_i) \in \mathbb{R}^p \times \mathcal{G}, i = 1, \ldots, n_t\}$ independent of L_n, where $(\tilde{x}_i, \tilde{y}_i)$ are independent realizations of v.a. with the same law as (X, Y). We then choose the sub-tree of $(T_j)_{1 \le j \le J}$ with index:

$$j^* = argmin_{1 \le j \le J} \{ \frac{1}{n_t} \sum_{i=1}^{n_t} (\tilde{y}_i - \hat{y}_{T_j,i})^2 \}, \qquad [3.10]$$

where $\hat{y}_{T_j,i}$ is the output associated with $\tilde{x}_i$.

As mentioned earlier, one of the advantages of decision trees is the readability and ease of interpretation of results, thanks to the tree graph that provides a natural understanding of the model. Another advantage is that this method can address raw data. Moreover, unlike generalized linear models, it is possible to take into account linearly related explanatory variables, and the link between the output variable and the other variables can be nonlinear.

However, this method has some disadvantages: for example, the models obtained are not particularly reliable because they depend largely on the learning sample. Minor changes in the learning base can significantly alter the model obtained. This is one of the reasons why decision trees are now used as blocks of more sophisticated methods using a large number of models in parallel: model aggregation methods (random forests, bagging, boosting) will be presented in section 3.5. We also note that the decision trees do not give an overall segmentation for each explanatory variable: it is possible for a variable to appear several times in different paths.

The CART method admits variants [BRE 84] and there are also other methods for constructing decision trees, such as the C4.5 algorithm introduced by Quinlan [QUI 93] and widely used within the IT community. It is also possible to construct predictors based on more regular recursive partitioning than decision trees, which define constant functions piecewise (see, for example, Friedman's [FRI 91] MARS algorithm).

Decision trees have applications in many fields. They can be used in actuarial science, for example, in non-life pricing, as the article by A. Paglia and M.P. Guinvarc'h [PAG 11] illustrates.

It should be noted that the CART algorithm is implemented in R language in the *rpart* package.

3.3. Neural networks

This section is an introduction to "neural networks" or "connectionist methods", which can be defined as the set of numerical problem-solving methods using models derived from neurobiology. The first major reflections were around 1940, and some names can be cited such as von Neumann, Turing, Wiener, McCulloch and Pitts. The objective then was to use the new knowledge brought by biology and cognitive sciences on the brain to design computer systems having some of its properties such as adaptive learning by successive local modifications and relocation of information storage, with the effect, for example, of robustness in cases of partial destruction. Two schools of thought emerged from these initial works. The first one (von Neumann, Turing, etc.) adopted a symbolic approach and was at the origin of concepts still used in our computers (memory, processors) and in "traditional" artificial intelligence. The second one (McCulloch, Pitts, Minsky, etc.) voluntarily followed a "connectionist" approach closer to biological description (neuromimetism). This approach saw a revival when the difficulties of traditional artificial intelligence came to light in the 1980s. The results have sometimes been spectacular and give rise today to highly advanced practical applications (forms and writing recognition, speech synthesis, time series prediction, medical diagnostic assistance, etc.), but the mathematical analysis of these nonlinear models remains very complex.

Neural networks constitute a vast field of research from a theoretical perspective and as regards applications (see, for example, the comprehensive book of K.-L. Du and M. Swamy [DU 14]). We will focus on layered networks and the well-known gradient backpropagation algorithm, which offer very interesting applications in supervised learning and are complementary methods to simpler and more conventional statistical models (linear and logistic regression). Recently, there has been renewed interest in these methods, followed by the development of even more efficient learning methods: deep learning, in particular, is already revolutionizing the world of artificial intelligence.

Note that the Kohonen algorithm and SVM methods, which will be presented in the subsequent sections, also derive their origins from neural modeling. The development of SVM, for example, was initially influenced by Rosenblatt's work on Perceptron in 1962 [ROS 62].

3.3.1. *From real to formal neuron*

One of the first neuromimetic constructions of the basic unit of neural computation is attributable to McCulloch and Pitts [MAC 43] in 1943. The real neuron, very schematically, works as follows:

– weighted summation of nerve impulses (inhibitors or exciters) from the neurons to which it is connected, via dendrites and synapses;

– emission in the axon of an influx if input summation exceeds an activation threshold.

McCulloch and Pitts' formal neuron reproduces these two properties. For an $x \in \mathbb{R}^p$ input, the unit of synaptic weights: $w \in \mathbb{R}^p$ and activation threshold: $\theta \in \mathbb{R}$ calculates:

– the weighted sum: $w.x = \sum_{i=1}^{p} w_i x_i$;

– the output $P_w(x) = \Phi(w.x - \theta) = \mathbb{I}_{\{w.x \geq \theta\}}$;

where the function $\mathbb{I}_{\{A\}}$ is 1 if A is real and 0 if not. The function Φ is called the activation function or the response function. We simplify the notations by posing $w_{l+1} = \theta$ and by considering an additional input: $x_{p+1} = -1$ such that we can write $P_w(x) = \mathbb{I}_{\{w.\tilde{x} \geq \theta\}}$, where $w.\tilde{x} = \sum_{i=1}^{p+1} w_i x_i$ and $\tilde{x} = (x_1, \ldots, x_{p+1})$.

Note that such a neuron carries out a function of $\mathbb{R}^p$ in $\{0,1\}$. There was no reason to limit oneself to Heaviside's response function of $\Phi(\mathrm{u}) = \mathbb{I}_{\{u \geq 0\}}$, and other functions have appropriately replaced it in many applications:

– $\Phi(\mathrm{u}) = u$ (linear neuron or Widrow–Hoff method);

- $\Phi_T(\mathrm{u}) = \frac{1}{1+exp(-\frac{u}{T})}$ called temperature T sigmoid, converging simply to $\Phi_0(\mathrm{u}) = \mathbb{I}_{\{u \geq 0\}}$ when $T \longrightarrow 0$. One of the advantages of this activation function, with respect to Heaviside's response function, is that it is continuous and differentiable everywhere, which will be essential for the majority of learning algorithms;

- $\Phi_{T,a,b}(\mathrm{u}) = \mathrm{a} + (\mathrm{b} - \mathrm{a})\, \Phi_T(\mathrm{u})$, sigmoid with values in $]a, b[$, in particular $\Phi_{T,-1,1}(\mathrm{u}) = \tanh(\frac{u}{2T})$.

These early works of McCulloch and Pitts gave birth to the connectionist school. However, it was not until 1960 that the first application was observed: Rosenblatt's [ROS 62] Perceptron. Introduced in 1962 by the psychologist Rosenblatt, the Perceptron designates a set of connected formal neurons. Rosenblatt's objective was to model the visual recognition of images, inspired by the biological structure of vision: the retina, the projection and associative areas are modeled by an input vector and successive layers of neurons connected to one another. We will see below that artificial multilayer neural networks reproduce this structure. Before studying neural networks, let us look at what functions the simple Perceptron, that is, the simple neuron of McCulloch and Pitts, can actually compute. We follow the historical approach of the connectionist school.

3.3.2. *Simple Perceptron as linear separator*

We focus on the function: $P_w(x) = \mathbb{I}_{\{w.\tilde{x} \geq \theta\}}$, from $\mathbb{R}^p$ to $\{0,1\}$, defined by the synaptic weights: $w \in \mathbb{R}^{p+1}$. Let us introduce the next notion.

DEFINITION.– *Two sets $A, B \subset \mathbb{R}^l$ are said to be linearly separable if there exists: $w \in \mathbb{R}^{p+1}$ such that:*

– *every x in A verifies: $\sum_{i=1}^{p} w_i x_i \geq w_{p+1}$;*

– *every x in B verifies: $\sum_{i=1}^{p} w_i x_i < w_{p+1}$.*

Similarly, a function $f : D \subset \mathbb{R}^p \longrightarrow \{0,1\}$ is said to be linearly separable if the sets $A = \{x \in D: f(x) = 1\}$ and $B = \{x \in D: f(x) = 0\}$ are linearly separable.

By definition, a given $f : D \subset \mathbb{R}^p \longrightarrow \{0,1\}$ function is linearly separable if and only if there exists a P_w function defined as above and such that $f(x) = P_w(x)$ for every $x \in D$.

Even by restricting ourselves to the case of the Boolean functions $f : \{0,1\}^p \longrightarrow \{0,1\}$, we do not know a general formula giving the number of linearly separable functions. The most famous example is the case $p = 2$: the logical functions and and or are linearly separable, while the function xor (or exclusive) is not. Indeed, the sets $A = xor^{-1}(1) = \{(0,1), (1,0)\}$ and $B = xor^{-1}(0) = \{(0,0), (1,1)\}$ are not separable by a straight line in $\mathbb{R}^2$. Note that this negative result (xor not computable by a simple Perceptron) was observed in 1969 by Minsky and Papert. Although they had also constructively demonstrated that a simple Perceptron can compute any linearly separable function, this result put an end for a time to the vogue of connectionism. If for small p it is easy to determine P_w realizing a given linearly separable Boolean function, it is not the same in a more general case. Rosenblatt established an algorithm that determines the coefficients w by a learning process.

Let A and B be two finite sets of $\mathbb{R}^p$, strictly linearly separable, that is, there exists $w^* \in \mathbb{R}^{p+1}$, such that $w^*.\tilde{x} > 0$ for every $x \in A$ and $w^*.\tilde{x} < 0$ for every $x \in B$, where $\tilde{x} = (x_1, \ldots, x_{p+1})$. Note that it is easy to show that the condition A and B being strictly linearly separable is equivalent to A and B being linearly separable. We are looking for a w^* vector carrying out this linear separation. The SPL (simple Perceptron learning) algorithm gives a solution.

We assume the set $A \cup B$ indexed, that is, $A \cup B = \{x(1), \ldots x(M)\}$.

SPL algorithm:

1) Initialize w: randomly choose $w(0)$ in $\mathbb{R}^{p+1}$.

2) $t := 0$; $test := 0$.

3) For $i := 1$ to M;

If $x(i) \in A$ and $w.\tilde{x}(i) \leq 0$, then $w(t+1) := w(t) + \tilde{x}(i)$; $test := 1$;

Else If $x(i) \in B$ and $w.\tilde{x}(i) \geq 0$, then $w(t+1) := w(t) - \tilde{x}(i)$; $test := 1$;

Else $w(t+1) := w(t)$;

End If.

$t := t + 1$.

End For.

4) If $test = 1$ go to 3.

End If.

5) End.

A priori, this algorithm may never stop. However, Minsky and Papert showed in 1969 that this is not the case and that the SPL algorithm converges in a finite time t, giving a vector $w(t) \in \mathbb{R}^{p+1}$, such that $w(t).\tilde{x} > 0$ for every $x \in A$ and $w(t).\tilde{x} < 0$ for every $x \in B$. The algorithm stops in a finite number of steps; however, in practice, convergence can sometimes be slow: Minsky and Papert showed that in the most unfavorable cases, the number of learning steps increases exponentially with the number of elements to be classified. There are possible extensions: for example, separation by a sphere and not a hyperplane, or classification no longer in two classes by a hyperplane but in several classes, or even determination of a hyperplane separating at best a set of nonlinearly separable points. However, Amaldi showed in 1991 that finding the largest linearly separable subset in a set that is not separable is an NP-complete problem, that is, there is no algorithm performing this task in a polynomial time.

3.3.3. *Multilayer Perceptron as a function approximation tool*

Let us introduce the mathematical formalism of layer structured neural networks, which are models very much used in practice in neural network approximation problems.

DEFINITION.– *Let* $p, m, q \in \mathbb{N}^*$, ϕ_c, ϕ_s *functions from* $\mathbb{R}$ *to* $\mathbb{R}$, $W^1 = (W_{ij}^1, i = 1, \ldots, p+1, j = 1, \ldots m)$ *and* $W^2 = (W_{jk}^2, j = 1, \ldots, m+1, j = 1, \ldots q)$ *real matrices.*

The function:

$$P(W^1, W^2, \ \phi_c, \ \phi_s): \mathbb{R}^p \longrightarrow \mathbb{R}^q$$

$$x \longmapsto s = (s_k = \phi_s(\textstyle\sum_{j=1}^{m} W_{jk}^2 \ \phi_c(\sum_{i=1}^{p+1} W_{ij}^1 x_i) - W_{m+1,k}^2), k = 1, \ldots q),$$

is called Perceptron with hidden layer synaptic weights (W_{ij}^1) *and* (W_{jk}^2) *of activation functions* ϕ_c *and* ϕ_s *with the convention:*

$$x_{p+1} = -1.$$

The activation functions are the same for all the units of the same layer, that is, ϕ_c for those of the hidden layer and ϕ_s for those of the output. In practice, these functions are generally the Heaviside step function, linear functions or sigmoid functions. However, we can imagine other choices such as trigonometric functions.

To simplify the notations, we have limited ourselves to the definition of a network with a hidden layer. This construction is easily generalized in the case of networks with several hidden layers. This idea is at the origin of deep learning methods (LeCun, Hinton, Bengio) (see, for example, the article by J. Schmidhuber [SCH 15]).

As early as 1969, Minsky and Papert showed that a multilayer network could surpass the limitations of the simple Perceptron. However, it was not until the works of Le Cun (1985), McClelland and Rumelhart (1986), including the famous learning algorithm of "gradient backpropagation" that the connectionist methods were actually used. This algorithm is in fact a generalization of an algorithm proposed by Widrow–Hoff (1960) and the gradient method used is a relatively classical method to solve variational problems in optimal control (Courant (1943), Kelley (1960), Dreyfus (1962), Bryson and Ho (1969) to name a few). This algorithm, which transforms the Perceptron from the classifier status (approximator of functions $\mathbb{R}^l$ in $\{0,1\}$) to that of universal approximator, will be justified mathematically by the results of Hornik (1989, 1992), Cybenko (1989) and Barron (1993), which show, for example, that any function of $\mathbb{R}^l$ in $\mathbb{R}^n$ having a finite number of discontinuities can be approached with arbitrary precision by some networks with a hidden layer. Let us set forth one of these fundamental theorems in the case of functions with values in $\mathbb{R}$ for a certain class of networks.

THEOREM.– *(Hornik, [HOR 93]) Let $I \subset \mathbb{R}$ be a non-empty interval. Let U in $\mathbb{R}^p$, and $\phi: \mathbb{R} \longrightarrow \mathbb{R}$ bounded Borel, non-polynomial on I.*

Let $\mathcal{P}(\phi, I, U)$ be the set of Perceptrons with a hidden layer from $\mathbb{R}^p$ to $\mathbb{R}$ with the form:

$$P(\theta, W^1, W^2)(x) = \sum_{j=1}^{m} W_j^2 \, \phi(\sum_{i=1}^{p} W_{ij}^1 \, x_i - \theta_j) \qquad [3.11]$$

where:

$m \in \mathbb{N}^*, W^2 \in \mathbb{R}^m, W^1 \in U^m$ *and* $\theta \in I^m$. *Let K be a compact set of $\mathbb{R}^p$.*

Therefore:

i) For every finite measure μ on K, $\mathcal{P}(\phi, I, U)$ is dense in all $\mathbb{L}^r(\mu), r \in [1, +\infty[$: for every $f \in \mathbb{L}^r(\mu)$ function, there exists a sequence $(f_k) \in \mathcal{P}(\phi, I, U)$, such that for every $\varepsilon > 0$, there exists $N \in \mathbb{N}$, such that for every $k \geq N$,

$$\|f - f_k\|_r = \left(\int_K |f(x) - f_k(x)|^r \, d\mu(x)\right)^{1/r} < \varepsilon. \qquad [3.12]$$

ii) As soon as ϕ is dx-almost surely continuous, $\mathcal{P}(\phi, I, U)$ is dense in the set $C(K)$ of continuous functions on K provided with the infinity norm $\| g \|_\infty = sup\{|g(x)|, x \in K\}$.

It is an existence theorem, demonstrated by convolution methods. This theoretical result is important, but gives no information on the size of the hidden layer (number of m units) that must be chosen to approximate a given function with a precision desired. There are however few theoretical results on the rate of convergence as a function of m. A typical example is the result of Barron (1993), which showed an approximation in the sense $\mathbb{L}^2$of the order $1/\sqrt{m}$ for a certain class of functions, but this result is not very useful in practice.

3.3.4. *The gradient backpropagation algorithm*

We will now focus on the algorithmic aspect of networks with a hidden layer within the framework of the approximation of functions by supervised learning. We will first present a regression problem and assume a known learning base $L_n = \{(x_i, y_i) \in \mathbb{R}^p \times \mathbb{R}^q, i = 1, \ldots, n\}$. We are looking for a Perceptron with a hidden layer comprising p inputs, q output units and a fixed m number of units in the hidden layer approaching at best the relationship between X and Y. Once the ϕ_c and ϕ_s activation functions are chosen, which are now assumed derivable everywhere, a Perceptron P is determined by the values of the weights $(\mathrm{W}_{\mathrm{ij}}^1)$ and $(\mathrm{W}_{\mathrm{jk}}^2)$. The approximation quality can be measured by the mean squared error function on the learning base:

$$\mathcal{E}_a\left((\mathrm{W}_{\mathrm{ij}}^1), (\mathrm{W}_{\mathrm{jk}}^2)\right) = \frac{1}{n}\sum_{i=1}^{n} \| y_i - P(W^1, W^2, \ \phi_c, \ \phi_s)(x_i) \|_2^2, \qquad [3.13]$$

where $\|.\|_2$ is the usual Euclidean norm on $\mathbb{R}^q$ and $\mathcal{E}_a$ is a function of $(p+1)m + (m+1)q$ variables $(\mathrm{W}_{\mathrm{ij}}^1)$ and $(\mathrm{W}_{\mathrm{jk}}^2)$, which we seek to minimize. In the case of a linear regression model, we can find a single explicit solution, because this minimization problem leads to the resolution of a linear equations system. This is no longer true in general; we use an iterative minimization method, the "gradient method".

Let us present the gradient or deeper descent method to determine a local minimum of a function $g: \mathbb{R}^l \longrightarrow \mathbb{R}$, of class C^1, reduced by a constant (g is positive in our case). Note: $\nabla g(z) = (\frac{\partial g}{\partial z_1}, \ldots, \frac{\partial g}{\partial z_l})(z)$ the gradient vector of g in z. The algorithm is as follows:

Gradient method algorithm:

1) Choose $z(0)$ in $\mathbb{R}^l$, such that $\nabla g(z(0)) \neq 0$, a sequence $(\eta(t) > 0, t \in \mathbb{N})$ and $\varepsilon > 0$.

2) t:=0.

3) $z(t+1) := z(t) - \eta(t) \nabla g(z(t))$; $t =: t + 1$.

4) If $|z(t) - z(t-1)| > \varepsilon$, go to 3.

End if.

5) End.

If the chosen parameter $\eta(t)$ is small enough, we have $g(z(t+1)) < g(z(t))$. Indeed, the Taylor series of g in $z(t+1)$ is written as:

$$g(z(t+1)) = g(z(t)) - \eta(t) \parallel \nabla g(z(t)) \parallel_2^2 + \eta(t)\, \epsilon(\eta(t)), \qquad [3.14]$$

where $\epsilon(u) \longrightarrow 0$ for $u \longrightarrow 0$. However, the choice of $\eta(t)$ is delicate: a too large value may cause oscillation phenomena around a minimum, whereas a too small value can make the convergence too slow. Many variants exist for the choice of η; we can consider the sequence $\eta(t)$ constant or decreasing towards 0 for $t \longrightarrow +\infty$.

In the gradient algorithm, we can also fix the number of learning steps rather than test the numerical convergence of the sequence $(z(t))$. Note that this algorithm may not converge to the global minimum if there are local minima. Various techniques exist (stochastic gradient for example) to try to escape the basins of attraction of these local minima.

Let us apply this algorithm to our minimization problem of $\mathcal{E}_a$. The gradient of $\mathcal{E}_a$ can be explicitly computed if the activation functions are derivable. We are then able to write a learning algorithm of a network with a hidden layer using the "gradient backpropagation" method (GBP).

GBP algorithm:

1) Set a learning base $L_n = \{(x_i, y_i) \in \mathbb{R}^p \times \mathbb{R}^q, i = 1, \ldots, n\}$, a number of learning steps M and learning constants $\eta(t), t = 1, \ldots, M$.

2) Initialize weights $W^1(0)$ and $W^2(0)$.

3) For $t = 1$ to M:

$$W_{ij}^1(t) = W_{ij}^1(t-1) - \eta(t)\frac{\partial \mathcal{E}_a}{\partial W_{ij}^1}(W^1(t-1), W^2(t-1)) \quad \text{for} \quad i = 1, \ldots, p+1, j = 1, \ldots, m$$

$$W_{jk}^2(t) = W_{jk}^2(t-1) - \eta(t)\frac{\partial \mathcal{E}_a}{\partial W_{jk}^2}(W^1(t-1), W^2(t-1)) \quad \text{for} \quad j = 1, \ldots, m+1, k = 1, \ldots, q$$

End For

4) End.

Some remarks and avenues can be explored from the literature:

– Here, the stop criterion is a fixed number of learning steps. In practice, learning is generally carried out in a hundred steps. We can imagine an additional or alternative condition on the error $\mathcal{E}_a$, for example, stopping the algorithm if $\mathcal{E}_a$ no longer varies (learning is finished). However, this latter condition is not always appropriate. The network can sometimes improve until it reaches a near-perfect modeling of the learning base, but subsequently prove unable to give suitable values on another sample: this is called "overlearning". To avoid this, we assume to know a finite disjoint set $V_{n_v} = \{(u_i, v_i) \in \mathbb{R}^p \times \mathbb{R}^q, i = 1, \ldots, n_v\}$ of L_n, called the "verification base". The observations (u_i, v_i) of V_{n_v} are assumed to be independent and derived from random variables of the same law as that of L_n. At each step t of learning on L_n, we also evaluate the mean squared error on V_{n_v}:

$$\mathcal{E}_v(\mathrm{t}) = \frac{1}{n_v}\sum_{i=1}^{n_v} \| v_i - P(W^1(t), W^2(t), \ \phi_c, \ \phi_s)(u_i) \|_2^2 \qquad [3.15]$$

In general, this error initially decreases over time, similar to what happens on L_n, and then stabilizes or increases when the network reaches the overlearning phase. This gives a stopping criterion for the learning algorithm: it suffices to stop when $\mathcal{E}_v(\mathrm{t})$ reaches its minimum. In addition, a third sample, disjoint of L_n and V_{n_v}, called "test base" or "validation", is often retained, on which the model selected after learning is tested. To be useful in prediction, the model must give an error of the same order on the three sets. A model that gives the best results on L_n will not always be the most highly-performing in prediction.

Overlearning is very sensitive to the complexity of the model and therefore to the number of hidden units: what are the links between the size of the network, the size of the learning base and the confidence that one can have in its generalization capacities? We can find theoretical results on learning in Vapnik and Chervonenkis (1971) [VAP 00], but the experimental results give much better results than theoretical bounds that impose gigantic learning bases to obtain correct generalization results. Some results were achieved: for a fixed-size learning corpus, the generalization error increases with the number of hidden neurons, because the network is progressively less constrained by the learning base. It is known in practice that, for equal performance, small networks tend to generalize better than large ones. By analogy, we can think of the approximation of real functions by polynomials: choosing high-degree polynomials is not always the best solution! There is always the dilemma between bias and variance: with a more complex model, we can gain precision on the learning set, but to the detriment of greater uncertainty in prediction. This is especially true if the variable to be predicted is poorly explained by the input variables. It is preferable to start with simple models, with m of a few units. In recent years, a theoretical approach to statistics has been developed, which makes it possible to obtain theoretical criteria for choosing the number of hidden units from a Perceptron with a hidden layer [RYN 12]. The choice of the "best" model is a delicate problem: comparing the models cannot be limited to comparing average risks, since the complexity of the different models must also be taken into account. Different statistical criteria have been developed, in particular for linear models (adjusted R^2, AIC and BIC, for example). It is also possible to use these criteria to compare different models of neural networks (see the articles by Ingrassia and Morlini [ING 05, ING 09] and Rynkiewicz [RYN 12]).

– The choice of ϕ_c and ϕ_s activation functions is directly related to the considered problem and to the nature of the data. In the case of regression, a current choice is the identity function for ϕ_s and the sigmoid function: $\Phi_T(\mathrm{u}) = \frac{1}{1+exp(-\frac{u}{T})}$ for ϕ_c. We can choose the fixed learning constant $(0.01 \leq \eta \leq 1)$ or slowly decreasing towards 0; for example: $\eta(t) = \lambda^t$, with $\lambda \approx 1, \lambda < 1$.

– As in data analysis, it is sometimes necessary to preprocess the data: for example, in the case of a classification based on numerical explanatory variables, it is preferable to center and reduce the variables if they are very disparate.

– The algorithm is easily generalized in the case of networks with several hidden layers. The method is the same, only the calculations are slightly complicated.

– There are many variants and extensions of this algorithm just as there are variants improving the gradient algorithm: conjugate gradient method, second-order methods (involving second partial derivatives of $\mathcal{E}_a$ relative to variables), Levenberg–Marquardt and Broyden–Fletcher–Goldfarb–Shanno methods, stochastic methods and method of moments for minimizing oscillations. In the latter case, the formula for modifying a weight $W_{ij}^l, l = 1,2$, is written as:

$$W_{ij}^l(t+1) = W_{ij}^l(t) + \Delta W_{ij}^l(t), \qquad [3.16]$$

where:

$$\Delta W_{ij}^l(t) = -\eta(t)\frac{\partial \mathcal{E}_a}{\partial W_{ij}^l} + \alpha(t)\Delta W_{ij}^l(t-1), \qquad [3.17]$$

with: $\alpha(t) > 0$.

– A method often used involves adding a regularization term in the function to be minimized. This then becomes:

$$\mathcal{E}_a = \frac{1}{n}\sum_{i=1}^{n} \| y_i - P(W^1, W^2, \ \phi_c, \ \phi_s)(x_i) \ \|_2^2 + \ \delta \ (\| W^1 \| + \| W^2 \|), \qquad [3.18]$$

where $\| W^l \|$ is a norm measuring the size of the matrix terms W^l. The parameter $\delta \geq 0$ (often called the decay parameter, since in a gradient algorithm, this term encourages the parameters to decrease towards 0) must be set by the user. This term favors small values of synaptic weights and aims to prevent the chaotic evolution of parameters during learning. It also limits the overlearning phenomena of highly noisy data. This is also justified by Bartlett's (1998) theoretical work (see [ING 05]).

– We can find many empirical recipes in the literature that attempt to mitigate the problem of local minima in the gradient algorithm. Here are a few examples, whose objective is a better exploration of the weight space: carrying out successive learning with various weight initializations, increasing episodically and abruptly the learning constant and adding a dose of noise to the weights.

– Another variant consists of modifying the weights between each presentation of an example of the base L_n (or by constructing successive subsets of L_n) and no longer by taking into account the entire base at each learning step. This is particularly useful when the learning base is very large.

Layer-structured neural networks may also be used in supervised classification: in the case of K classes classification problem with p input variables, it is possible to consider a neural network with p inputs having K output units, such that the output vector of the model is standardized with the softmax function: the jth output value is defined by:

$$S_j(x) = \frac{exp(s_j(x))}{\sum_{k=1}^{K} exp(s_k(x))}, j = 1,\dots,K$$

where $s_j(x)$ is the value given by the jth output neuron. This normalization makes it possible to obtain at the output a vector that can be interpreted as being a probability vector. By recoding the different classes in the complete disjunctive form, the class k is identified with the vector $\vec{e}_k = (0,\dots,0,1,0,\dots,0)$ of $\mathbb{R}^K$ (with 1 in the kth position) and learning is performed by minimizing the cross-entropy H or the relative entropy $\widetilde{H}$: for a learning set $L_n = \{(x_i, y_i) \in \mathbb{R}^p \times \{\vec{e}_1, \dots \vec{e}_K\}, i = 1,\dots,n\}$,

$$H(W) = -\sum_{i=1}^{n} \sum_{k=1}^{K} y_{i,k} \, log(S_k(x_i)), \quad [3.19]$$

$$\widetilde{H}\,(W) = \sum_{i=1}^{n} \sum_{k=1}^{K} y_{i,k} \, log(y_{i,k}/S_k(x_i)), \quad [3.20]$$

to which can be added a parameters control term (for example, $\delta \parallel W \parallel$, W designating the set of parameters of the model), as with the mean squared error function. Once the learning is complete, the prediction of the class associated with an observation x is then:

$$\hat{k}(x) = \{k \in \{1,\dots,K\} : S_k(x) = max_{j=1,\dots,K} S_j(x)\}. \quad [3.21]$$

Some examples of the application of supervised learning in multilayer networks include: the recognition of forms and, in particular, speech and handwriting recognition [HAS 09] and the automatic reading of postal codes (US Post Office, 1989); voice synthesis (Nettalk, 1986); classification of radar, sonar and seismic signals; time series prediction (for example, daily consumption of water or electricity [TOC 95] or series of financial market data with a change in regime [MAY 04]); business failure prediction (see P. du Jardin's essay and his very numerous bibliographical references on this subject [DU 07]); medical diagnosis [CHA 05]; data processing and actuarial modeling (classification based on customer databases in the banking and insurance sectors (see, for example, articles by A. Paglia and M. Phelippe-Guinvarc'h [PAG 11], JM Aouizerate [AOU 12] and the actuarial dissertation by E. Le Corre [LEC 12]). This list is not exhaustive, but shows the diversity of fields of application. By their nonlinear nature, neural methods allow us to approach complex problems to which there is no analytical solution. In a way, we simulate a complex system by another complex system, but artificial neural methods are capable of learning and controllable by adjustment of parameters.

These methods are implemented in R language in *VR* packages (or *nnet*), *AMORE, neuralnet* and *h2o*.

3.4. Support vector machines (SVM)

Support vector machines (SVM) constitute a class of supervised learning algorithms initially defined for the discrimination between two classes. They were then generalized for multiclass problems and for the prediction of quantitative variables. In the case of discrimination between two classes, they are based on the search for an optimal margin hyperplane, separating as best as possible the two subsets of observations. Here, we find the principle of the simple Perceptron (section 3.3.2), with the idea of seeking an optimal solution, the best one to generalize.

This method's approach stems from Vapnik's work in the theory of statistical learning from 1995 on the links between the complexity of a model and its generalization capacities [COR 95, VAP 00].

3.4.1. *Linear separator*

3.4.1.1. *Maximum margin separator hyperplane*

When the observations are linearly separable, we have seen that Rosenblatt's simple Perceptron and the associated learning algorithm make it possible to determine the equation of a separating hyperplane. We will elaborate this notion by seeking an optimal solution and we shall see that this notion can be extended to the nonlinear case.

Let us consider a learning set $L_n = \{(x_i, y_i) \in \mathbb{R}^p \times \{-1, +1\}, i = 1, \dots, n\}$, where y_i indicates to which of the two classes belongs the individual characterized by the variables $x_i = (x_{i,1}, \dots x_{i,p})$.

We provide $\mathbb{R}^p$ with a scalar product, denoted by ".". A hyperplane H of $\mathbb{R}^p$ is defined by its equation: $w.x + b = 0$, where w is a vector orthogonal to H.

The set of elements of L_n is said to be linearly separable if there exists a vector $w \in \mathbb{R}^p$, with $\| w \| = 1$ and a constant $b \in \mathbb{R}$, such that the inequalities below are verified for $i = 1, \dots, n$:

$$w.x_i + b \geq 1, \text{ if } y_i = 1, \text{ and } w.x_i + b \leq -1, \text{ if } y_i = -1.$$

This is equivalent to $y_i(w.x_i + b) \geq 1$, for $i = 1, \dots, n$. In this case, the sign of $f(x) = w.x + b$ indicates in which side of the hyperplane the point x is and also the class associated with x.

The choice of the constant 1 is arbitrary since a hyperplane is defined within a multiplicative constant. There are an infinite number of solutions: we seek that of the maximum margin, that is, the hyperplane, which is as far as possible from all the examples. We call the margin the distance between the two respective equation hyperplanes $w.x + b = -1$ and $w.x + b = 1$.

We confound a vector w and the coordinate point w without the risk of confusion. The signed distance from a point x to a hyperplane H of equation $w.x + b = 0$ is $d(x, H) = (x - w_1).w_0$, where w_1 is the unique point of H such that the vector w_1 is collinear to the vector w and $w_0 = w/\| w \|$. Since the point w_1 belongs to H, we have $w_1.w_0 = -b/\| w \|$, where:

$$d(x, H) = (x.w + b)/ ||w|| = f(x)/ ||w||. \quad [3.22]$$

Since the function f is equal to -1 and $+1$ on the hyperplanes forming the edges, we deduce that the margin associated with the hyperplane H is equal to $2/ ||w||$. To obtain the maximum margin, we therefore have to minimize the function $\Phi(\mathrm{w}, \mathrm{b}) = \| w \|$ (or in an equivalent manner $\| w \|^2$) under the constraints $y_i(w.x_i + b) \geq 1$, for $i = 1, \dots, n$.

For this, we use the Lagrange multiplier standard method. Thus, the Lagrangian:

$$L(w,b,\alpha) = \frac{1}{2}\, w.w \; - \sum_{i=1}^{n} \alpha_i \, (y_i(w.x_i + b) - 1), \qquad [3.23]$$

where α is the vector of the Lagrange multipliers $\alpha_i \geq 0, i = 1,\ldots,n$. The solution to our problem is determined by the saddle point (w^*, b^*, α^*) of the Lagrangian in the dimensional space $n + p + 1$ corresponding to the variables w, α and b, taking the minimum relative to p coordinates of w and b and the maximum relative to $\alpha_i, i = 1,\ldots,n$. At the point realizing the minimum (in w and b), we have:

$$\left\{\frac{\partial L(w,b,\alpha)}{\partial w}\right\}_{w=w^*} = w^* - \sum_{i=1}^{n} \alpha_i \, y_i \, x_i = 0, \qquad [3.24]$$

$$\left\{\frac{\partial L(w,b,\alpha)}{\partial b}\right\}_{b=b^*} = -\sum_{i=1}^{n} \alpha_i \, y_i \; = 0 \qquad [3.25]$$

Substituting these conditions in the Lagrangian, we obtain:

$$L(w^*, b^*, \alpha) = \sum_{i=1}^{n} \alpha_i - \frac{1}{2}\, w^*.w^* \; = \; \alpha.u \; - \; \frac{1}{2}\, \alpha D \alpha^T, \qquad [3.26]$$

where $u = (1,1,\ldots,1) \in \mathbb{R}^n$, α^T is the transpose of α (that is, the column vector) and D is the symmetric matrix: $D = (D_{ij} = y_i y_j x_i . x_j)_{i,j=1,\ldots n}$. Thus, to find the saddle point, it is necessary to determine the maximum in α of:

$$\tilde{L}(\alpha) = L(w^*, b^*, \alpha) = \; \alpha.u \; - \; \frac{1}{2}\, \alpha D \alpha^T, \qquad [3.27]$$

under the constraints $\alpha.y = 0$ and $\alpha \geq 0$, where $y = (y_1,\ldots,y_n)$. According to the Kuhn–Tucker optimization theorem, at the saddle point (w^*, b^*, α^*), each Lagrange multiplier α_i^* and the corresponding constraint are linked by the equation:

$$\alpha_i^* \; [\, y_i \; (x_i . w^* + b^*) - 1] = 0, \;\; i = 1,\ldots,n. \qquad [3.28]$$

In other words, $\alpha_i^* \neq 0$ only for the examples of L_n such that the inequality $y_i(w.x_i + b) \geq 1$ is an equality. These points, x_i, for which $y_i(w.x_i + b) = 1$, are called "support vectors", and the above condition

$\frac{\partial L}{\partial w} = 0$ shows that the solution w^* is written as a linear combination of these support vectors:

$$w^* = \sum_{i:\, \alpha_i^* \neq 0} \alpha_i^* \, y_i x_i. \qquad [3.29]$$

The resolution of this mean square optimization problem then provides the equation of the optimal hyperplane $w^*.x + b^* = 0$, with $b^* = -\frac{1}{2}\,[w^*.x^+ \; + \; w^*.x^-]$, where x^+ and x^- are support vectors of each class.

It is then possible to use the separating hyperplane obtained to make the prediction: for a new observation x presented to the model, the sign of the function $f(x) = \; w^*.x + b^*$ gives the class to attribute to it.

3.4.1.2. *The nonlinearly separable case*

When the observations are not separable by a hyperplane, it is necessary to relax the constraints by introducing ξ_i error terms that control their overrun:

$$y_i(w.x_i + b) \geq 1 - \xi_i \,, \; i = 1, \ldots, n. \qquad [3.30]$$

The model thus assigns a false response to a vector x_i if the corresponding ξ_i is greater than 1. We are then brought back to the problem of minimization of the function:

$$\Psi(w, b, \xi) = \frac{1}{2} w.w \; + \; \delta \sum_{i=1}^{n} \xi_i, \qquad [3.31]$$

under the constraints $y_i(w.x_i + b) \geq 1 - \xi_i$ and $\xi_i \geq 0$ for $i = 1, \ldots, n$, where δ is a strictly positive parameter. The method using the Lagrange multipliers still works in this case (see, for example, [COR 95]).

Note that many algorithms exist to solve the mean square optimization problems, in the separable case or not. Some, proposing a decomposition of the learning set, are more particularly adapted to take into account a significant number of constraints when the number of observations n is large.

3.4.2. *Nonlinear separator*

When the observations are not linearly separable, it is sometimes possible to find a nonlinear boundary. An astute way to approach this problem is to notice that it is often possible to make these observations linearly separable by considering their images by a nonlinear application K in a space $\mathcal{G}$ with dimension greater than that of the initial space $\mathcal{F} = \mathbb{R}^p$.

Moreover, since the method used in the linearly separable case will only involve scalar products $y.y'$ for vectors y and y' with the form $y = \mathrm{K}(x)$ and $y' = \mathrm{K}(x')$, it is not necessary to explain the function K, if we know a symmetric function $k : \mathcal{F} \times \mathcal{F} \longrightarrow \mathbb{R}$ called *kernel* such that:

$$k(x, x') = \mathrm{K}(x).\mathrm{K}(x'). \qquad [3.32]$$

Mercer's condition ensures that a symmetric function $k(.,.)$ is a kernel if for all possible x_i, the general term matrix $k(x_i, x_j)$ is a positive definite matrix, that is, it defines a scalar product matrix. In this case, we show that there exists a space $\mathcal{G}$ and a function $\mathrm{K} : \mathcal{F} \longrightarrow \mathcal{G}$, such as: $k(x, x') = \mathrm{K}(x).\mathrm{K}(x')$. Examples of commonly used kernels include:

– degree d polynomial kernel: $k(x, x') = (c\ x.x')^d$, with $c \in \mathbb{R}$;

– hyperbolic tangent kernel: $k(x, x') = tanh(c_1\ x.x' + c_2)$, with $c_1, c_2 \in \mathbb{R}$;

– Gaussian (or radial) kernel: $k(x, x') = exp(-\frac{\|x - x'\|^2}{2\,\sigma^2}), \sigma^2 > 0$.

The SVMs were then extended to the case of several classes and are developed in several R packages: *e1071, kernlab, klaR* and *svmpath* (see the article by Hornik *et al.* [HOR 06] for the presentation of these packages).

3.5. Model aggregation methods

In the previous sections, we have presented different methods of supervised learning, which offer a multitude of possible models, but it is often difficult to know which one to retain. Rather than selecting just one of these models, the general principle of aggregation methods (or ensemble methods) is to construct a collection of predictors and then aggregate all of their predictions. In regression, the final prediction may be an average of the predictions given by the different models, whereas within the framework of classification, we can proceed with a majority vote among the classes provided by the various predictors. This technique is only of interest if the different basic models selected give significantly different results, which is the case for nonlinear methods such as decision trees and neural networks for example, which have less bias than linear methods on complex problems, but a higher variance. The aggregation of different models then makes it possible to reduce the variance and thus the instability of basic models. The basic models can be of different natures, but the methods using decision trees have been the most developed, including specifically "random forests". We will now present the usual aggregation methods, focusing on two categories:

– parallel methods that bring together basic models constructed independently of each other, such as bagging and random forests;

– adaptive methods where each basic model included in the model depends on the previous one and is constructed according to the latter's performance on the learning set. These methods are known as boosting.

These different methods are being used in actuarial science, particularly in property and casualty insurance, for predicting individual claims amounts, fraud detection or development of zones (see, for example, [LEB 16]).

3.5.1. *Bagging*

The bagging method was introduced by Breiman [BRE 96]. The word bagging is a contraction of the words bootstrap and aggregating. Given a learning sample L_n and a basic method, the bagging principle is to independently draw B bootstrap samples $L_{n,1},\ldots,L_{n,B}$ in L_n, to calibrate the basic method on each of them to construct B predictors $\hat{\phi}_1(.),\ldots\hat{\phi}_B(.)$. The final estimator is then:

– $\hat{\phi}(.) = \frac{1}{B}\sum_{b=1}^{B}\hat{\phi}_b(.)$, in regression;

– $\hat{\phi}(.) = argmax_j\ card\{b : \hat{\phi}_b(.) = j\}$, in classification.

In the first case, it is simply the average value of the different estimates, and in the second case, a majority vote on the B predictions.

Two techniques are generally used to generate bootstrap samples:

– the samples $(L_{n,b})$ are obtained by drawing n observations with replacement in L_n, each observation being drawn with $1/n$ probability;

– the samples $(L_{n,b})$ are obtained by drawing l observations (with or without replacement) in L_n, with $l < n$.

Bagging makes it possible to render weak basic methods more effective. This was demonstrated mathematically on a particular example by Biau and Devroye [BIA 10]: taking the 1-nearest neighbor method as the basic method (which is not universally consistent) and bootstrap samples with size l_n such as $\lim_{n\to\infty} l_n = +\infty$ and $\frac{\lim_{n\to\infty} l_n}{n} = 0$, they demonstrated that the asymptotic bagged estimator $\tilde{\Phi}(.) = \lim_{B\to\infty} \frac{1}{B}\sum_{b=1}^{B} \hat{\Phi}_b(.)$ is universally consistent.

It is possible to use an out-of-bag method to estimate the error in prediction of the model obtained on a test sample: this makes it possible in particular to check how this error evolves as a function of B, in order to choose a sufficient number of basic models. In the case of bagging, it is not necessary to have an additional sample independent of L_n. In effect, not all basic models contain all observations. To obtain a learning-independent prediction for an observation (x_i, y_i) of L_n, we therefore limit ourselves to the set $\mathcal{M}$ of basic models that do not use this observation to be calibrated, and the prediction associated with x_i is then:

$$\hat{y}_i = \frac{1}{card(\mathcal{M})} \sum_{b\in\mathcal{M}} \hat{\Phi}_b(x_i). \qquad [3.33]$$

In a classification context, we proceed with majority vote. The out-of-bag error is then defined by:

– $\frac{1}{n}\sum_{i=1}^{n}(y_i - \hat{y}_i)^2$ in regression;

– $\frac{1}{n}\sum_{i=1}^{n} \mathrm{I}_{\hat{y}_i \neq y_i}$ in classification.

In order to simplify, assuming that all the basic predictors have as theoretical variance σ^2 and that two basic predictors constructed by the bootstrap method have as correlation coefficient ρ, then it is easy to see that the predictor obtained by bagging has as variance $\rho\sigma^2 + \frac{(1-\rho)\sigma^2}{B}$. Thus, it appears that the variance decreases with the number B of basic models used and also that the correlation between the basic models quantifies the gain of the aggregation procedure: the more decorrelated the basic models are (small $|\rho|$), the smaller the variance of the final model will be. This stands as a justification for taking basic models sensitive to the learning sample, such as trees or neural networks: otherwise, the basic models will be strongly correlated and aggregating them will not result in any improvement.

Bagging is very easy to program. There is an R package, *ipred*, which offers efficient implementations of this method.

3.5.2. *Random forests*

In the case of CART models, Breiman [BRE 01] proposed an improvement in bagging by the addition of randomization. The aim is to make the basic models less correlated by adding randomness in the choice of variables used in the different basic models. We have seen the value in the preceding section: using less correlated basic models helps to reduce the predictor variance obtained by aggregation. To this end, Breiman proposed to randomly select, at each stage of the construction of a tree, m variables among the p explanatory variables and to determine the corresponding split by taking only these variables into account. Note the $L_n = \{(x_i, y_i) \in \mathbb{R}^p \times \mathcal{G}, i = 1, \dots, n\}$ learning set, where $\mathcal{G} = \mathbb{R}$ in the case of regression and $\mathcal{G} = \{1, \dots, K\}$ in that of classification. The algorithm is as follows:

Random forest algorithm:

1) Choose $B, m \in \mathbb{N}^*$.

2) For b = 1 to B:

– *draw a Bootstrap sample* $L_{n,b}$ *in* L_n*;*

– *with the sample* $L_{n,b}$*, construct a CART tree, which defines a predictor* $\hat{\phi}_b(.)$*. Each split of the tree is determined by restricting to a set of* m *variables randomly drawn among the* p *explanatory variables, the draws being independent for the different splits.*

End For

3) Define $\hat{\phi}(.) = \frac{1}{B}\sum_{b=1}^{B} \hat{\phi}_b(.)$ (or $\hat{\phi}(.) = argmax_j\, card\{b : \hat{\phi}_b(.) = j\}$).

The value of this approach has been demonstrated when the number of p explanatory variables is very significant (see, for example, [CAR 08]). The number of randomly drawn variables m can be a sensitive parameter. The classical choices are $m = \sqrt{p}$ in classification and $m = p/3$ in regression. This is the default choice in the R *randomforest* library. As with bagging, the out-of-bag error evaluation is used to control the value of B and possibly to optimize the value of m.

Since its publication in 2001, this method has been extensively studied and used, due to its very good prediction qualities (see, for example, the comparative article by M. Fernandez-Delgado *et al.* [FER 14] and the article by Biau and Scornet [BIA 16a]). From a theoretical point of view, convergence results, which are difficult to obtain, were demonstrated in 2015 by Scornet *et al.* [SCO 15]. Also note the recent article by Biau *et al.* [BIA 16b], which establishes an interesting link between random forests and neural networks.

3.5.3. *Boosting*

The boosting method was introduced in 1996 by Freund and Schapire [FRE 96], and it has a common characteristic with bagging in that it uses basic models to deduce a final predictor by aggregation. However, the essential difference is that boosting constructs the basic models iteratively and adaptively, in order to gradually correct the mistakes made. The initial idea was to improve the performance of models having performance barely better than a random classifier for predicting a binary variable. This resulted in the AdaBoost algorithm [FRE 97], which is the most popular boosting algorithm. Let us note $L_n = \{(x_i, y_i) \in \mathbb{R}^p \times \{-1,1\},\ i = 1,\dots,n\}$ learning set. The algorithm is therefore as follows:

AdaBoost algorithm:

1) Choose $M \in \mathbb{N}^*$.

2) *Initialize the weights:* $w = (w_i = 1/n, i = 1, \dots n)$.

3) For m = *1 to M*:

- adjust a basic model $\hat{\phi}_m(.)$ on weighted L_n by the weights $w_1, \dots, w_n$;
- calculate the apparent error rate on L_n for the model $\hat{\phi}_m(.)$:

$$\mathcal{E}_m = \frac{\sum_{i=1}^{n} w_i \mathrm{I}_{\{y_i \neq \hat{\phi}_m(x_i)\}}}{\sum_{i=1}^{n} w_i}$$

- calculate: $\alpha_m = log((1 - \mathcal{E}_m)/\mathcal{E}_m)$;

- modify the weights: $w_i = w_i\ exp(\alpha_m \mathrm{I}_{\{y_i \neq \hat{\phi}_m(x_i)\}}), i = 1, \ldots n$;

End For

4) Define: $\hat{\phi}(.) = sign(\sum_{m=1}^{M} \alpha_m\ \hat{\phi}_m(\cdot))$.

All the observations are equally weighted for the first model; then, at each iteration, the weight of an observation remains unchanged if it is well classified and increases otherwise. The final predictor is a weighted aggregation of the basic models, the weighting being a function of the adjustment qualities of each model. Basic models may be weak, but it should be ensured in practice that they are better than a random predictor (one in two chances of being mistaken): we must have $\mathcal{E}_m > 0.5$, otherwise α_m becomes negative.

The basic model calibration step with the weights $(w_1, \ldots, w_n)$ offers several possibilities. For example, weights w_i can be used to weigh the empirical error to be minimized:

$$\frac{1}{n}\sum_{i=1}^{n} w_i \mathrm{I}_{\{y_i \neq \hat{\phi}_m(x_i)\}}$$

The basic model can also be adjusted on a subsample of size n of L_n, by randomly drawing observations (with replacement) according to the weights $(w_1, \ldots, w_n)$.

The AdaBoost algorithm has been widely used with CART trees as basic models. It has also been extensively studied from a theoretical perspective (see, for example, the article by Bartlett and Traskin [BAR 07], which shows properties of universal consistency).

Multiple variations have also been proposed to adapt it to the case of multiclass or quantitative output variables (see, for example, [SCH 01]). In 1997, Drucker proposed a version of boosting for regression (see, for example, [GEY 06] for performance analysis in the case of CART trees).

Note: $L_n = \{(x_i, y_i) \in \mathbb{R}^p \times \mathbb{R}, i = 1, \ldots, n\}$ learning set. Drucker's algorithm is as follows:

Boosting algorithm for regression:

1) Choose $M \in \mathbb{N}^*$.

2) Define: $p_1 = (p_{1,i} = 1/n, i = 1, \ldots n)$. The uniform law on $\{1, \ldots, n\}$.

3) For m = 1 to M:

- draw an $\bar{L}_n$ sample of size n with replacement in L_n following the law p_m;
- adjust a basic model $\hat{\phi}_m(.)$ on $\bar{L}_n$;
- calculate on L_n for model $\hat{\phi}_m(.)$:
- $l_m(i) = Q\left(y_i, \hat{\phi}_m(x_i)\right)$ for i = 1, ..., n, where Q is a loss function;
- $\mathcal{L}_m = sup_{i=1,\ldots,M}\, l_m(i)$;
- $d_m(i) = \frac{l_m(i)}{\mathcal{L}_m}$;
- $\mathcal{E}_m = \sum_{j=1}^{n} p_{m,j}\ l_m(j)$;
- $\beta_m = \frac{\mathcal{E}_m}{\mathcal{E}_m - \mathcal{L}_m}$;
- if $\mathcal{E}_m < 0.5\, \mathcal{L}_m$, then define $w_{m+1,i} = {\beta_m}^{1-d_m(i)} p_{m,i}$;
- Otherwise define $w_{m+1} = p_1$.
- modify the probabilities: $p_{m+1,i} = w_{m+1,i} \,/ \sum_{j=1}^{n} w_{m+1,j}\,, i = 1, \ldots n$

End For

4) Calculate $\hat{\phi}(.)$, mean or median of weighted $\hat{\phi}_m(.)$ predictions by the coefficients $(log(1/\beta_m), m = 1, \ldots, M)$.

In this algorithm, the loss function Q can be quadratic, exponential or the absolute value, the usual choice in regression being the quadratic function. In the last step, the use of the median eliminates the influence of overly atypical predictors [GEY 06].

In 1999, Breiman proposed to consider boosting as a global optimization algorithm. According to this idea, Hastie *et al.* showed that the binary case can be seen as an approximation method by a stepwise constructed additive model, the algorithm minimizing an exponential loss function defined on the learning base (see [HAS 09]). This principle was developed by Friedman under the acronym MART (multiple additive regression trees) and then under the acronym GBM (gradient boosting machine) [FRI 01]. As for the AdaBoost algorithm, it is an issue of iteratively constructing a series of models such that the successive models improve and the final aggregation provides a good solution. The contribution of the GBM is that the successive modifications are determined by applying a gradient optimization method on a loss function Q to be minimized (see [FRI 01] or [HAS 09] for details).

GBM algorithm – Boosting by functional gradient descent:

1) Choose $\in \mathbb{N}^*,\ \lambda \in]0,1]$.

2) Define: $\hat{\phi}_0(.) = argmin_c \frac{1}{n}\sum_{i=1}^{n} Q(y_i, c)$

3) For m = *1 to M:*

- calculate the opposite of the gradient $-\frac{\partial}{\partial z}Q(y,z)$ at the points $z_i = \hat{\phi}_{m-1}(x_i)$. Let us note these values $(u_1, \ldots, u_n)$;

- adjust a basic model $\widehat{\Psi}_m(.)$ on $\{(x_1, u_1), \ldots, (x_n, u_n)\}$;

- deduce a new model $\hat{\phi}_m(.) = \hat{\phi}_{m-1}(.) + \lambda\widehat{\Psi}_m(.)$.

End For

4) The output is the model $\hat{\phi}_M(.)$.

The choice of the parameter λ is relatively insignificant. It is often recommended to take it in the order of 0.1. This choice is related to that of the optimal number of iterations: a small λ value will require a large number of iterations and vice versa.

The boosting algorithm is implemented in R in the *gbm* and *h2o* packages.

3.5.4. *Stacking*

Stacking (also called blending) is an approach that involves using as input to a statistical learning algorithm the output values given in a first step by different models. This is therefore a metamodel, which aggregates basic models in a more complex way than does the bagging method. The original idea was developed by Wolpert [WOL 92], and this method was then adopted in many applications. A particular case is where the metamodel is a linear model, whereas the basic models are nonlinear, such as neural networks or trees (see, for example, [BRE 96a]). In classification, a logistic regression model can be used as a metamodel to combine the predictions of basic models of different types (logistic regression, decision tree, neural network, etc.). This method is therefore relatively old but has proved very efficient in solving complex problems, such as the competition proposed on the Kaggle website (see, for example, [SIL 01] regarding the Netflix Prize).

The stacking method is implemented in the R *h2oEnsemble* package.

3.6. Kohonen unsupervised classification algorithm

The analysis of multidimensional data typically focuses on the study of n individuals determined by p variables (quantitative or qualitative): an individual is an element of a p-dimensional space.

The factorial methods (ACP and derivatives), which are in fact methods of projection of the linear algebra, allow graphical "representations" of the data in dimensions 1, 2 or 3. It is however difficult to construct proximity classes from projections if the individuals are not represented without loss of information in a dimensional space ≤ 3. Two individuals whose projections are close are not always close in the initial p-dimensional space.

On the other hand, the following two families of "classification" methods can be distinguished:

– hierarchical classification: iterative aggregation process of the nearest-neighbor classes. Initially, each individual is a class. We consider the n classes and group the two closest classes (for a chosen distance) to form a new class (of two individuals). And we iterate on the $n-1$ obtained classes until a single class is obtained. This gives rise to a representation by a tree.

We can then choose the number of classes that seems better adapted by selecting a grouping level;

– non-hierarchical classification: the number of classes is fixed *a priori* and one class is attributed to each individual by an algorithm converging towards a distribution minimizing the intra-class inertia (that is, the sums of distances of each individual of a class to the center of the class). A classic example is the moving average algorithm.

For these classification methods, two points of the same class are close in the initial space, but how can the classes be globally represented while preserving the initial topology of the data? There is no notion of neighborhood of classes.

Kohonen algorithm attempts to match representation and classification. In 1982, Teuvo Kohonen [KOH 82, KOH 96] proposed an algorithm whose main function is to match the elements of inputs space with ordinate units on a map giving a graphic representation (of dimension 1, 2 or 3), where each unit is surrounded by its neighbors (for a predefined distance). The result is a function of the input space to the set of units, such that the images of two neighboring elements in the sense of a certain distance in the input space are the same unit or neighboring units on the map.

Even if the algorithm proposed by Kohonen may only be considered as an unsupervised classification algorithm, it is initially related to neural modeling. It was conceived in 1982 as a modeling of the automatic formation of maps in the sensory areas of the cortex, although since then the mathematical study of the algorithm and its applications in particular in data analysis have distanced it from its original biological framework. For example, let us consider the nerve connections of retinal cells towards the cerebral cortex processing visual information (the tectum). If we imagine the retina as a grid of two dimensions, an important fact is that the topology of the retina is preserved by the set of connections in the sense that two close cells on the retina are connected to two close cells in the cortex. There is no reason for this to happen spontaneously at birth, and we may assume that this phenomenon is due to self-organization and selection process governed by the spontaneous activities of cerebral neurons. It is precisely this idea that T. Kohonen wanted to adapt when he defined his self-organization algorithm, adding an important concept to previous connectionist models that he knew very well (associative memory models of D. Gabor, J.

Hopfield, etc.). From an algorithmic point of view, the self-organization process is carried out by a local updating of connections according to complementary rules of competition and cooperation, at each presentation of a prototype.

3.6.1. *Notations and definition of the model*

The data space is a convex bounded subset $\chi \subset \mathbb{R}^p$, provided with the Euclidean distance. We consider a sample $(x(1),\ldots,x(t))$ from successive observations in χ (statistical approach) or realizations of a sequence of independent random variables of the same probability law μ with values in χ (probabilistic approach).

The network is formed of n units (or neurons) arranged according to a determined topology:

– with $d = 1, 2$ or 3 dimensions: a line, a square or a cube;

– according to a mesh whose neighborhood structure is determined by a neighborhood function. The units are represented by a subset I of $\mathbb{Z}^d$, and the neighborhood function is a Λ function defined on $I \times I$, which is:

- symmetric (that is, $\Lambda(i,j) = \Lambda(j,i)$),
- depending only on a distance $\mathcal{D}$ on I,
- decreasing with the distance: $\Lambda(i,j) \longrightarrow 0$ when $\mathcal{D}(i,j) \longrightarrow \infty$.

It is often agreed that $\Lambda(i,i) = 1$.

When $\Lambda(i,j) = 1$, we say that i and j are strongly connected, and when $\Lambda(i,j) = 0$, i and j are totally disconnected and have no interactions.

Each unit i is provided with a state vector $W_i(t) \in \mathbb{R}^p$ pointing in the data space, and can be modified. The state of the network at instant t is given by $(W_i(t),\ i \in I)$.

The objective is to find W_i vectors having properties of:

– quantification: the number of W_i vectors in a region A of χ is approximately proportional to $\mu(A)$;

– organization: two close units i and j (that is, $\Lambda(i,j) \approx 1$) have close W_i and W_j vectors.

Once such W_i vectors are determined, they are used to define the class of any $x \in \chi$ element: we attribute to x the class i^* such that:

$$i^*(x, W) = argmin\{\| x - W_i \|, i \in I\}, \quad [3.34]$$

where $\|.\|$ is a norm on $\mathbb{R}^p$. Let us now study the Kohonen algorithm, which determines W_i vectors by a learning method.

3.6.2. *Kohonen algorithm*

It is an iterative learning algorithm that modifies the W_i state vectors depending on the data presented to it:

– the vectors $W_i(t = 0)$ are randomly initialized;

– if at the instant $t \in \mathbb{N}$, the state of the network is given by $W(t) = \{W_i(t), i \in I\}$, then the state at the instant $t + 1$ will be determined as follows: an $x(t + 1)$ vector of the data space χ is randomly chosen.

The "competition phase" then appoints the winning unit:

$$i^*(x(t+1), W(t)) = argmin\{\| x(t+1) - W_i(t) \|, i \in I\}. \quad [3.35]$$

In the case where several units minimize this distance, one rule is agreed upon, for example, the first index i for the lexicographic order on $\mathbb{Z}^d$.

The "cooperation phase" modifies the W_i vectors:

$$\forall j \in I, W_j(t+1) = W_j(t) - \varepsilon_t \Lambda_t(i^*, j)\,(W_j(t) - x(t+1)), \quad [3.36]$$

where Λ_t is a neighborhood function, which can be time dependent, and $\varepsilon_t \in]0,1[$ is an adaptation parameter.

The algorithm is continued as long as t is less than a threshold value M fixed *a priori*, or else an alternative or additional stop condition can be imposed, which stops the algorithm if there is no appreciable improvement. The essential parameters of the algorithm are the dimension p of the data space, probability law μ (which characterizes the way in which the observations are distributed in the data space), network topology, neighborhood function Λ_t, constant or time-dependent, and the adaptation parameter ε_t, with values in $]0,1[$, which may be constant or decreasing in t.

The neighborhood function plays a significant role here: only the units close to the winning unit i^* have their W_i vector significantly modified: hence the notion of cooperation. Here are some common examples of neighborhood function:

– $\Lambda_t(i,j) = \begin{cases} 1, & si\ \mathcal{D}(i,j) \leq k \\ 0, & otherwise \end{cases}$ (where k is a fixed value, for example: $k = 1$ or $k = 2$);

– $\Lambda_t(i,j) = g(\mathcal{D}(i,j))$, where g is a bell-shaped function;

– $\Lambda_t(i,j) = g(\mathcal{D}(i,j)/\lambda(t))$, where $\lambda(t) \longrightarrow 0$, when $t \longrightarrow \infty$.

A common example is: $\Lambda_t(i,j) = exp(-\mathcal{D}(i,j)^2/2\sigma(t)^2)$, where:

– $\sigma(t) = \sigma_i\ (\sigma_f\ /\ \sigma_i\ )^{(t/M)}$, with $\sigma_i > \sigma_f > 0$ (for example, $\sigma_i = 5$ and $f = 0.2$).

The adaptation parameter ε_t plays a significant role in the convergence of the algorithm. For example, we can choose ε_t such that $\sum_{t\geq 0} \varepsilon_t = +\infty$ and $\sum_{t\geq 0}(\varepsilon_t)^2 < +\infty$, as $\varepsilon_t = 1/t$ (Robbins–Monro conditions derived from stochastic algorithms).

Another common example is: $\varepsilon(t) = \varepsilon_i\ (\varepsilon_f\ /\ \varepsilon_i\ )^{(t/M)}$, with $\varepsilon_i > \varepsilon_f > 0$ (for example, $\varepsilon_i = 0.1$ and $\varepsilon_f = 0.005$).

Analysis of the convergence of this algorithm poses difficult mathematical problems. Although the vast majority of the Kohonen algorithm applications use at least dimension 2 data spaces and show the phenomenon of self-organization, the great majority of mathematical results satisfactorily describing it are only valid in dimension 1 (string topology and dimension 1 data space)! For an overview of known mathematical results, reference can be made to the synthesis article by M. Cottrell, J.C. Fort and G. Pagès [COT 98]. This article also contains a very extensive list of references on the subject.

3.6.3. *Applications*

This algorithm and its numerous variants have a wide range of applications. In particular, the article [COT 03] can be consulted, where some examples are presented: analysis and comparison of countries identified by socioeconomic variables; electricity consumption curves; demography in municipalities of the Rhone valley; consumer profiles in Canada; segmentation of the labor market in France, etc. The advantage of this classification method is that it makes it possible to graphically represent the observations while respecting the network topology. The observations belonging to this class are thus associated with each unit. When the data and classes are very numerous, it is possible to carry out a second classification on the vectors representing the classes, in order to obtain a coarser classification level, which will be easier to interpret.

Many variants of this algorithm have been proposed. In particular, it is possible to apply it in the case of qualitative variables, by associating it with a factorial correspondence analysis [COT 03].

The Kohonen algorithm is particularly implemented in the R *kohonen* package.

3.7. Bibliography

[AOU 12] AOUIZERATE J.M., "Alternative neuronale en tarification santé", *Bulletin Français d'Actuariat*, no. 23, pp. 97–127, 2012.

[BAR 07] BARTLETT P., TRASKIN M., "Adaboost is consistent", *Journal of Machine Learning Research*, no. 8, pp. 2347–2368, 2007.

[BIA 10] BIAU G., DEVROYE L., "On the layered nearest neighbour estimate, the bagged nearest neighbour estimate and the random forest method in regression and classification", *Journal of Multivariate Analysis*, no. 101, pp. 2499–2518, 2010.

[BIA 16a] BIAU G., SCORNET E., "A random forest guided tour", *TEST*, no. 25, pp. 197–227, 2016.

[BIA 16b] BIAU G., SCORNET E., WELBL J., "Neural random forests", *arxiv:1604.07143*, 2016.

[BRE 84] BREIMAN L., FRIEDMAN J.H., OLSHEN R.A. *et al.*, *Classification and Regression Trees*, Wadsworth Advanced Books and Software, Belmont, 1984.

[BRE 96a] BREIMAN L., "Stacked regressions", *Machine Learning*, no. 24, pp. 49–64, 1996.

[BRE 96b] BREIMAN L., "Bagging predictors", *Machine Learning*, no. 26, pp. 123–140, 1996.

[BRE 01] BREIMAN L., "Random forests", *Machine Learning*, no. 45, pp. 5–32, 2001.

[CAR 08] CARUANA R., KARAMPATZIAKIS N., YESSENALINA A., "An empirical evaluation of supervised learning in high dimensions" *Proceeding of the 25th International Conference on Machine Learning*, New York, United States, 2008.

[CHA 05] CHAKRABORTY S., GHOSH M., MAITI T. *et al.*, "Bayesian neural networks for bivariate binary data: an application to prostate cancer study", *Statistics in Medicine*, no. 24, pp. 3645–3662, 2005.

[COR 95] CORTES C., VAPNIK V., "Support-Vectors networks", *Machine Learning*, no. 20, pp. 273–297, 1995.

[COT 95] COTTREL M., GIRARD B., GIRARD Y. *et al.*, "Neural modeling for time series: a statistical stepwise method for weight elimination", *IEEE Transaction on Neural Networks*, no. 6, pp. 1355–1364, 1995.

[COT 98] COTTREL M., FORT J.C., PAGÈS G., "Theoretical aspects of the SOM algorithm", *Neurocomputing*, no. 21, pp. 119–138, 1998.

[COT 03] COTTREL M., IBBOU S., LETREMY P. *et al.*, "Cartes organisées pour l'analyse exploratoire des données et la visualisation", *Journal de la Société Française de Statistique*, no. 144, pp. 67–106, 2003.

[DU 07] DU JARDIN P., Prévision de la défaillance et réseaux de neurones: l'apport des méthodes de sélection de variables, PhD thesis, University of Nice, 2007.

[DU 14] DU K.-L., SWAMY M., *Neural Networks and Statistical Learning*, Springer, London, 2014.

[FER 14] FERNANDEZ-DELGADO M., CERNADAS E., BARRO S., "Do we need hundreds of classifiers to solve real world classification problems?", *Journal of Machine Learning Research*, no. 15, pp. 3133–3181, 2014.

[FRE 96] FREUND Y., SCHAPIRE R., "Experiments with a new boosting algorithm", *Proceeding of the 13th International Conference on Machine Learning*, Bari, Italy, 1996.

[FRE 97] FREUND Y., SCHAPIRE R., "A decision-theoritic generalization of online learning and an application to boosting", *Journal of Computer and System Sciences*, no. 55, pp. 119–139, 1997.

[FRI 91] FRIEDMAN J.H., "Multivariate adaptative regression splines", *The Annals of Statistics*, no. 19, pp. 1–67, 1991.

[FRI 01] FRIEDMAN J.H., "Greedy function approximation: a gradient boosting machine", *The Annals of Statistics,* no. 29, pp. 1189–1232, 2001.

[GEY 06] GEY S., POGGI J.M., "Boosting and instability for regression trees", *Computational Statistics and Data Analysis*, no. 50, pp. 533–550, 2006.

[HAS 09] HASTIE T., TIBSHIMARI R., FRIEDMAN J., *The Elements of Statistical Learning: Data Mining, Inference and Prediction*, Springer, New York, 2009.

[HOR 06] HORNIK K., KARATZOGLOU D., MEYER D., "Support vector machines in R", *Journal of Statistical Software,* no. 15, pp. 1–28, 2006.

[HOR 93] HORNIK K., "Some new results on neural networks approximation", *Neural Networks*, no. 6, pp. 1069–1072, 1993.

[ING 05] INGRASSIA S., MORLINI I., "Neural network modeling for small datasets", *Technometrics*, no. 47, pp. 297–311, 2005.

[ING 09] INGRASSIA S., MORLINI I., "Computational studies with equivalent degrees of freedom in neural networks", *Advances and Applications in Statistics*, no. 13, pp. 49–81, 2005.

[KOH 82] KOHONEN T., "Analysis of a simple self-organizing process", *Biological Cybernetics*, no. 44, pp. 135–140, 1982.

[KOH 96] KOHONEN T., *Self-Organizing Maps*, 2nd edition, Springer-Verlag, Berlin, 1997.

[LEB 16] LE BOUCHÉR B., Tarification I.A.R.D. et Open Data, Thesis, Institut des Actuaires, 2016.

[LEC 12] LE CORRE E., Constitution de groupes homogènes de risque dans le cadre de solvabilité II, Thesis, Institut des Actuaires, 2012.

[MAC 43] MCCULLOCH W., PITTS W., "A logical calculus of the ideas immanent in nervous activity", *Bulletin of Mathematical Biophysics*, no. 5, pp. 115–133, 1943.

[MAI 04] MAILLET B., OLTEANU M., RYNKIEWICZ J., "Nonlinear analysis of schocks when financial markets are subjects to change of regime", *Proceeding of XIIth European Symposium on Artificial Neural Networks (ESANN 2004)*, Bruges, Belgium, 2004.

[PAG 11] PAGLIA A., PHELIPPE-GUINVARC'H M., "Tarification des risques en assurance non-vie, une approche par modèle d'apprentissage statistique", *Bulletin Français d'Actuariat,* no. 22, pp. 49–81, 2011.

[QUI 93] QUINLAN J.R., *C4.5: Programs for Machine Learning*, Morgan Kaufmann, San Francisco, 1993.

[ROS 62] ROSENBLATT F., *Principles of Neurodynamics: Perceptrons and the Theory of Brain Mechanisms*, Spartan Books, Washington, 1962.

[RYN 12] RYNKIEWICZ J., "General bound of overfitting for MLP regression models", *Neurocomputing*, no. 90, pp. 106–110, 2012.

[SCH 01] SCHAPIRE R., "The boosting approach to machine learning. An overview", *MSRI Workshop on Nonlinear Estimation and Calibration*, Berkeley, United States, 2001.

[SCH 15] SCHMIDHUBER J., "Deep learning in Neural Networks: an overview", *Neural Networks*, no. 61, pp. 85–117, 2015.

[SCO 15] SCORNET E., BIAU G., VERT J.P., "Consistency of random forests", *The Annals of Statistics*, no. 43, pp. 1716–1741, 2015.

[SIL 01] SILL J., TAKACS G., MACKEY L. *et al.*, "Feature-weighted linear stacking", *arxiv:0911.0460*, 2001.

[VAP 00] VAPNIK V., *The nature of Statistical Learning Theory*, Springer-Verlag, New York, 2000.

[WOL 92] WOLPERT D., "Stacked generalization", *Neural Networks*, vol. 5, no. 2, pp. 241–259, 1992.

4

Current Vision and Market Prospective

4.1. The insurance market: structured, regulated and long-term perspective

In France, the insurance market is essentially composed of large companies, often of international size, powerful and strong, offering to private clients and companies the guarantee of solvent and sustainable third parties and the ability to appropriately address disasters and financial crises. In general, these companies are old, resulting from combination of structures often created more than a century ago, or subsidiaries of large banking groups.

Several types of structures coexist: for-profit limited insurance companies, mutual insurance companies with non-profit civil society status, provident institutions and mutual insurers. Traditionally specialized in individual health insurance, many mutual insurers have grouped together or moved closer to provident institutions specialized in health and collective welfare insurance for corporate clients. Regrouping trends have also affected provident institutions and there are now only a handful of groups, which may also include public limited companies.

Since the implementation of the Solvency II prudential regulation, which applies to all of these structures' activities, historical differences in governance are partially erased, although differences in culture and values remain as well as mutual insurers and provident institutions, for example, not having, the initial vocation to select policyholders.

Chapter written by Florence PICARD.

4.1.1. *A highly regulated and controlled profession*

Insurance business requires an authorization. The authorization is issued by the (ACPR) Autorité de contrôle prudentiel et de resolution (Prudential Supervision and Resolution Authority) after reviewing a file providing all the project's details, which must guarantee the financial strength (shareholders and business plan) as well as the skills of the management team. Authorization agreements are rare. However, in October 2016, an authorization was granted to a new digital insurance company, Alan, which offers health coverage primarily targeting start-up clients and whose main shareholder is CNP Assurances. However, in general, entrepreneurs wishing to invest in the insurance market are encouraged to work as brokers to build offerings, find clients and bring them to already existing insurers, which then bear the risk in their balance sheets in a prudential manner.

Insurance companies play a fundamental economic role. They allow companies to take risks, over time smooth the cost of accidents that can disrupt their operations and deal with serious claims that they would not be able to bear without the security provided by the insurers. Similarly, for individuals, they offer a pooling of everyday life risks (car, fire, disease, etc.) which, by spreading the cost of accidents on a large number of people, in space and time, makes it acceptable for everyone.

They are major financial actors. A significant part of French savings is entrusted to them, via life and death insurance contracts, whose funds are invested in the stock markets, in particular for the financing of national debt. They are also entrusted by public authorities with the collection of several taxes and solidarity levies, such as those intended to supply the compensation fund, for which a fixed amount is deducted from each property insurance contract. Clients are often unaware of this: they often assimilate these levies to management fees or price increases, which does not contribute to the readability of the prices or to a kind impression as regards the insurers.

Given the importance of the economic role played by insurance institutions regarding society, such institutions are highly regulated and monitored. They are strongly capitalized and follow the European Solvency II prudential regulation. They are subject to multiple laws and regulations, many of which are intended to ensure clients that the insurer will meet their obligations. Furthermore, the regulations aim at protecting insured persons such that insurers do not abuse clients' information, which they acquire by virtue of their occupation. Insurers are assumed to be placed in a situation of information asymmetry that gives them a position of strength relative to clients and are therefore limited to using pricing criteria. The regulations also stipulate that the use of personal data must be carried out whilst respecting privacy, without discrimination, in a parsimonious and equal manner, and that the insurer will take all the necessary security measures to protect themselves from data theft or leakage, under penalty of severe sanctions.

The role of actuaries is to make judicious use of data relevant to risk assessment and control, including the calculation of claims provisions. The data quality must have been previously verified.

Insurance companies are mainly controlled by the Prudential Supervision and Resolution Authority (ACPR), which carries out close supervision of their activities, supported by frequent and highly documented reporting. The organization and governance of insurance companies are supervised by the ACPR. The appointment of executives and key functions officials (actuarial function, risk management, compliance and audit) is subject to declarations and authorizations from the ACPR.

As major data users, insurance companies are also in frequent contact with the CNIL (National Commission on Informatics and Liberty) through their CIL (Data Protection Correspondent) and now their DPO (data privacy officer), a function that must have been created around May 2018, with a deadline for compliance with the GDPR, the General Data Protection Regulation.

4.1.2. *A wide range of long-term activities*

The guarantees issued by insurance companies cover all economic fields: coverage of property held by individuals or companies, coverage of the consequences of natural events, civil liability insurance, health, retirement, death and welfare insurance as well as life insurance and savings, etc.

Their exploits fall within a long-term perspective, particularly for pension and personal protection insurance as well as public liability insurance, especially product and construction insurance. With regard to retirement, in view of survivor pension, the duration of a contract can exceed one century.

As a result, insurers are required to manage product portfolios, with old contracts still active, while, over time, new contracts, more adapted to changing needs, are added to the existing portfolios.

The strength and solidity of insurance companies are therefore inseparable from a certain amount of management burden, with layers of processes and computer devices that are difficult to absorb, especially as, on the one hand, these insurers are the result of numerous mergers of companies, and on the other hand, tax and social regulations are constantly changing, which renders processing more complex.

The wide range of areas of insurance practice actually corresponds to different trades, with distinct markets and often different distribution channels.

Personal insurance is sold to a large extent as B2C (business to consumer), but client contact is not always the responsibility of the insurance company. Traditional companies (Axa, Allianz, Aviva, etc.) offer many distribution channels: employee networks that directly link the client with the insurer, as well as general agents who act with a certain independence on behalf of the insurer for which they are agents, and also brokers who have an autonomy of action, put insurers in competition and provide personalized advice, and independent asset management advisors (IAM) who place savings contracts and intervene in the arbitrage of financial supports. However, individuals can also turn to the banking networks that distribute the contracts of insurance companies, which are subsidiaries of banks. These companies which have recently come into existence now account for two-thirds of the life insurance market and the growing shares of car and home insurance for individuals.

All these companies as well as their distributors have telephone platforms including sites and online sales as well as smartphone applications, with sale means increasingly appreciated by the French for all their expenditures.

Henceforth, multichannel marketing must enable clients to use all means of information and advice on products, including all modes of distribution. Clients want to be able to use all these channels to inquire, receive advice and buy, when they desire, with the need to be recognized everywhere, with all their history, including the most recent one, regardless of the different distribution channels used and the different insurance areas covered. Thanks to Hamon law, nowadays individuals can change insurers more easily. They are helped in this regard by the rapid growth of comparators that allow them to have a global vision of the market and find the offer and price best suited to their needs. Concerning corporate clients, certain lines of insurance that require a technical approach, such as companies' operating risks, resort to underwriter engineers with advanced skills in the insured domain.

The commercial approaches, guarantees offered and skills adapted to the various insurance domains and to the different client segments are therefore varied and equally require a wide variety of organizations and methods.

4.1.3. *A market related to economic activity*

Insurance supports and secures entrepreneurs and individuals in their activities. The market volume is thus linked to that of the activities. With regard to the economic context, the French market is generally mature in a large number of sectors, notably the volume of property insurance: car and home insurance. In car insurance, the tendency of urban youth to opt for one-time rental rather than the purchase of a vehicle is not neutral for insurers if it is confirmed. This reduces the market and switches it from B2C to B2B (business-to-business and fleet contracts with renters).

4.1.4. *Products that are contracts: a business based on the law*

Regarding contractual relationships between the insurer and their client, it is the law that governs mutual obligations. In property insurance, the contract is established for a given period by the signing of documents describing the object of the insurance and the insurer's commitments on the basis of the insured's declarations. If a claim occurs during the insurance period, the insurer must fulfill their obligations on the basis of this contract.

Insurers are often criticized for writing disclaimers of warranties and other important details as minor items. Insurers attempt to remedy this, but the very nature of the transaction, which takes the form of a contract, that is, a legal act, and not a tangible object, which makes it difficult to be simplified. The contracts of Anglo-Saxon digital actors are more burdensome and incomprehensible than insurance contracts, but the service is immediate and usually free, which simplifies the relationship, even if, with time, clients get "committed", often without their knowledge.

This undeniable legal dimension of the insurance business is a handicap in the client's experience that needs to be overcome.

4.1.5. *An economic model based on data and actuarial expertise*

Although privately owned, insurance companies play a fundamental role in social utility, particularly for health and welfare contracts, in addition to compulsory schemes. They are therefore subject to incentives or constraints from public authorities, through fiscal or regulatory measures.

In health insurance, for example, the tax rate is differentiated depending on whether the health contracts are qualified as responsible or not responsible, whilst taking into account the fact that it is the public authorities who define the terms of reference and the basket of care that the contracts must conform with in order to be validated as "responsible".

Obviously, clients mostly choose contracts with the most competitive prices, that is, responsible contracts, since they are less taxed.

In other cases, by laws or regulations, for reasons of non-discrimination or for the sake of solidarity, the insurer's pricing freedom is limited by the prohibition of the use of certain criteria, such as gender, although it is quite discriminating in terms of life expectancy, or regarding medical history, via the right to oblivion which prevents it from being taken into account.

The insurance business, which consists of a promise to pay an amount, usually unknown, if a random event occurs in the future, is based on statistics. This information is carefully collected and stored in structured databases. The pooling of different clients' risks allows the insurer to rely on the law of large numbers to model its own risk by mathematical laws of probability using a few criteria summarizing most of the information. It also measures the risk of error of this modeling, which is used by the regulator to pronounce its capital mobilization requirement with respect to the promises of coverage made by insurers. Data is therefore the raw material for insurers. It is the job of the actuaries to choose and use them to assess and control risks, and calculate the provisions to be entered in the accounts while prospectively and stochastically projecting over several years into the future the various technical and commercial parameters to ensure the company's sustainability and commitments. So far with a limited amount of data, insurers have effectively assessed their risks and have, in due course, faced the promised regulations in the event of disasters. It is obvious that the explosion of the digital industrial revolution data we know, called big data, comes to shake this established order.

What is the usefulness of this new large amount of data for insurers?

4.2. Big data context: new uses, new behaviors and new economic models

It is a banality to observe the digital explosion and big data phenomenon characterized by the 5Vs: volume, variety, velocity, veracity and value.

The most visible manifestation of big data is the explosion of the "volume" of data, exponentially growing due to the power of computers and the generalization of the Web, smartphones, social networks, connected objects, cloud accessibility, etc.

However, big data also profoundly modifies the context by the "variety" of data exchanged: numbers of course, as well as text, image, sound and video. Another characteristic is "velocity", the speed at which information instantly and simultaneously reaches all corners of the planet, emanating from all sorts of issuers, individuals sending their vacation photos or collecting claims information by satellite. In the digital age, everything is instantaneous and the technologies made available to individuals become quite similar to those of companies.

"Veracity" remains a focus point because data is collected without knowledge of their context, and this must be kept in mind in the uses that are subsequently made of it. All these data, shared using new algorithms and artificial intelligence, constitute the new source of energy of the 21st century, generating “value”.

All economy actors are making great efforts towards extracting value from all these data, taking their share of the enrichment and succeeding in their digital transformation, notably towards taking advantage of this new data for marketing purposes.

4.2.1. *Impact of big data on insurance companies*

How are insurance companies affected by big data? What impact does the digital world have on the activities of insurers?

Due to their original economic model, the reverse cycle, insurers are particularly concerned by this digital industrial revolution since data is their raw material. In view of an expensive random event (a disaster), an individual or a company has the choice between taking up the challenge to take the risk and incur the cost or deciding to transfer that risk to a trusted third party for an initial paid price. Vendors of “promises”, who have been carefully evaluated based on proven methods regarding the use of statistics, are data professionals who convert individual risks that are difficult to bear into a controlled overall risk. In this regard, the provision of new data can only help insurers to do their job better.

But is the impact of digital technology not of a very different nature? Is it not in the process of not only modifying the way the insurance business is exercised, but also insurance business itself?

Insurance activities support economic and financial activities and are therefore largely dependent on these activities. They are at the service of individuals to help them face the dangers of their way of life. If the economy changes and people live differently, insurance needs will be different too.

Insurance companies must therefore understand and adapt to changing needs and even anticipate them.

4.2.2. *Big data and digital: a profound societal change*

Big data and the ongoing digital industrial revolution are bringing about a profound societal change.

Each individual has become the node of a network and all networks are interconnected. This increase in the volume of communication speeds up time. A mail must be processed during the day. Exchanges take place through mobiles, tweets and other ultra-short message systems. Information is quickly outdated. This is done by headlines and shocking images that leave little room for feature articles, nuanced and argued exchanges. Everything goes fast. We no longer bear waiting. The site must give the information quickly without requiring a long questionnaire. The product must be delivered the same day or the next day. We live in the present instant, without much projection into the future. Digital speeds up time.

And we get used to the service of digital platforms like Amazon, which look after their "client experience" and set the bar high for traditional actors.

The insurer's long time and its reverse cycle do not naturally fit into this new world of the present moment. The insurer's rare traditional contact opportunities with clients (contributions and claims) cannot allow them to meet their needs adequately. To exist, one must be in contact. Therefore, the insurer will seek for contact opportunities and the digital will provide it: site, smartphone alerts, etc.

In some ways, the development of comparators favored by digital technology and the measures taken by public authorities to facilitate competition, which put insured persons in a position of choice, give insurers new contact and market promotion opportunities. However, insurers' client experience is more difficult to achieve than for a product seller because of the reverse cycle, which delays the "delivery of the product", which the client will not really want to receive since it would mean that a disaster has happened.

In the context of economic crisis and declining purchasing power, as well as ecological awareness, individuals are seeking consumer solutions, rather than the possession of the useful object. The "vélib'" flourish in many cities as well as the "Autolib'". Have we permanently entered into a society of usage more than property? In any case, clients, natural persons or legal entities increasingly pay attention to prices, at times to the detriment of quality.

However, price has lost its economic value significance. Digital has accustomed individuals to "free" Google, Facebook and other services, and settlement is being done indirectly by the free input of all user data, which are then the subject of an intense commercial activity. It also allowed airlines and SNCF (National Society of French Railways) to charge very different prices depending on the filling rate at the time of booking (and sometimes other more questionable criteria), which may lead to passengers traveling together, under the same conditions, whilst paying prices ranging from 1 to 10. Users no longer have any reference and are tempted to think that big companies make excessive margins, waste and charge too much and that it is always possible to find lower prices. On the one hand, users are better informed about market insurance rates by comparators and about their own risk through open data (or soon to access their genome); on the other hand, they no longer have stable references on prices, the formation of which they do not understand. Reducing information asymmetry between clients and insurers, brought about by digital technology, does not really enhance confidence.

In this new digital world, pampered by platforms and armed with their smartphone, individuals are becoming aware of their power: with a feeling of complete power, they give their opinion by tweet regarding television programs, act as journalists by filming news scenes and directly question politicians. Somewhat like teenagers, they have more confidence in unknown Internet users, in forums or platforms, than in recognized specialists.

This partly explains the success of so-called "collaborative" platforms (BlaBlaCar, Airbnb, etc.) that bring individuals together for the exchange of services: car-pooling, lending houses or garden tools, as well as the temporary rental of apartments, cars, etc. The economic argument is also strongly put forward since it has been calculated that the economic gain of a collaborative economy would bring an average of € 495 to each.

Thanks to a relaxation of regulations, this collaborative economy has also reached financial activities, such as crowdfunding.

Some consumers are also starting to get rid of platforms by relying on both blockchain technology and social networks. Calling into question experience, skills and institutions, there are emerging trends among Internet users to organize themselves via peer-to-peer networks. Communities are created and, thanks to social networks, collective intelligence and blockchain technology, they are planning transactions that were until entrusted to trustworthy third parties that are regulated and controlled by public authorities. In the United States, a community of this type, peer-to-peer dynamics, proposes to carry out the unemployment insurance of a community via LinkedIn. Another one, "Teambrella", is interested in the car insurance coverage of its members and determines the insurance price and entry of new members by vote.

After the time of B2C (business to customers) and B2B (business to business), is this the time of C2C (consumer to consumer)?

4.2.3. *Client confidence in algorithms and technology*

The public is developing the habit of having to deal with robots and is properly adapting to it: automatic cashouts, airports, banks, supermarkets, automatic subways. Algorithms are considered more reliable than humans and many prefer to be guided by a robot than a human. The robot, which is never tired, has no physiological needs or moods and no emotions need to reassure it. Due to its rationality, it is even perceived as objective, even though it has been coded by humans and depends on the culture they transmitted to it, which differs, especially from one continent to another. The algorithm is not objective. On the contrary, it risks being normative and impose criteria and values.

The confidence individuals have in technology also concerns encryption technologies: the Bitcoin blockchain appears to be totally safe and the code is law for the Ethereum blockchain which says everything in the way some humans now rely on technology rather than institutions. Thanks to technology, some prefer trust shared with strangers rather than with institutions – "trusted third parties" – established for centuries. This tendency to discredit, which affects all institutions, notably politicians and journalists, does not spare banks and insurers, although it is not yet reaching them head-on.

This tendency is partially offset by the need for human contact in some purchasing processes (despite the growing purchase of consumer products online). In insurance, there has been an increase in the need for contact with a manager to manage a claim.

Moreover, resistance is beginning to emerge with regard to "black boxes", as shown, for example, by the protest movement concerning the post-bac APB algorithm for the allocation of students to universities.

4.2.4. *Some sort of negligence as regards the possible consequences of digital traces*

This loss of confidence in "institutions" contrasts with the lack of mistrust regarding the possible use of digital traces left by connected objects and via platforms as well as with regard to cyber risk. These connected objects develop, although they may take a while to start.

The connected Apple Watch, for example, regularly progresses and is now sold more than Swatch watches. Bank cards, store cards, Navigo passes, web browsing, smartphones, connected cars, geolocation, connected meters, alarms, home automation, medical objects, etc. trace their users in a sustainable manner without apparently moving them.

Yet the multiplication of traces and their crossing, especially with deep-learning, makes everyone traceable, even those who are not very active on digital networks, because they are networked with others who are connected. It suffices, for example, to have a parent or friend who is a Facebook user, so that via deep learning, Facebook can know everything about us, our tastes, our interests, our habits, etc.

Until now, digital technology has been developing without the public expressing too much fears of misuse of the masses of information that are permanently provided. Similarly, it is only recently that there is an emerging awareness of the value of data freely provided in exchange for free services as well as the economic imbalance of this exchange and that some voices are being raised to claim a remuneration.

However, in France, the data are not the property of the persons concerned. They are subject to regulations similar to those of the authorities and therefore cannot be sold by the persons themselves. On the contrary, paradoxically, these data can be traded elsewhere.

4.2.5. *New economic models*

Digital technology has brought in new actors (Amazon, La Fourchette, TripAdvisor, Uber, etc.), which, by interposing between the producer and the client and offering clients an irreproachable and personalized service, cut off the producer from their clients. Once installed, these platforms reduce the producer to a subcontractor role and make the law on prices, reducing producers' margins without always actually reducing prices for consumers.

Today, all economic actors are increasingly worried about being "uberized" as it was done, at varying extents, with taxi drivers, booksellers and restaurateurs. Insurance companies also fear the arrival of new digital actors, namely insurance "ubers" or "free", which would bring both a drop in prices and an agile digital service, not hampered by the historical weight of complex portfolios.

Insurance companies understand that clients do not want to "pay for others", that high-performing platforms have accustomed them to personalization of service and they want to find it in all their suppliers. They closely observe and often associate with Fintech and Insurtech, which flourish under the creative impulse of millennia, those young graduates who embark on their business, ready to hasten everything, far from the comfort and constraints of their elders' careers in the large corporations.

For insurance companies, the issue is to analyze the opportunities and risks of the new digital context of our big data world and to define their strategic approach in this rapidly changing universe.

4.3. Opportunities: new methods, new offers, new insurable risks, new management tools

Insurers are data professionals. On a technical level, to ensure solvency and meet commitments, their risk assessment is based on the observation of past results and sets of hypotheses for the future in a meticulous hypothetico-deductive approach. The stochastic models used by actuaries, including the generalized linear model (GLM), are hypothesis-driven. The Solvency II prudential regulation is itself based on these methods, and the ACPR regulator exercises its control over the data and used internal models and requires interpretability.

The conventional statistical and probabilistic methods of actuaries are therefore far from being obsolete.

4.3.1. *New data processing methods*

In big data world, new methods enrich the capacities of risk assessment, construction of offers and contacts with clients.

The approach is different from that of modeling. The number of variables is too high to be able to apply the same techniques. However, these are not *a priori* selected variables, but newly available existing data, which will often prove to be of no explanatory value in the subject under study. However, the work precisely consists of detecting cases where these new data are explanatory or predictive and it is in these situations that the data add value. To extract relevant information from large masses of data, it is therefore necessary to view the data from a data-driven perspective, with learning algorithms: decision trees, neural networks, random forests and even unsupervised classification algorithms.

Actuaries knew some algorithms of this type but so far, before big data, they had few opportunities to use them. Neuronal algorithms and classification methods were valuable for refining homogeneous pricing groups. However, they were only used on internal, numerical data from subscriptions, claims or other internal data databases, which limited their predictive power.

Data-driven is thus a new approach to data, without *a priori*, which helps to discover unsuspected correlations and proximities. However, we should not forget the business experience, especially as correlation does not equal causality. It is important to understand the context in order to properly use big data and algorithms. In this respect, due in particular to its reverse cycle and different relationship to time, the insurer's business differs from many of big data businesses. Algorithm results must be interpretable and it must be possible to explain the decisions taken.

Unlike many leading-edge activities in big data, most traditional insurance activities, apart from interactions with clients, do not require instant processing in the nanosecond. At present, it is rarely the rapidity of processing that takes priority over the interpretability of results. Within the framework of current insurance contracts, which are concluded for fairly long terms, usually 1 year, the scope of prediction falls within a much longer timescale than in most digital businesses, and situations are less repetitive than those of e-commerce actors.

Even with mass data, input data have limitations and must be taken into account at the output level. Letting the data speak does not mean letting algorithms do the work and taking the result without thinking. To take a simple example, if a machine learning algorithm study is based on a history of data from a socio-occupational profession that was closed to women, it should not be surprising that the prediction would contain a gender criterion even though this criterion will not be relevant in the prediction, given the initial bias.

Big data does not dispense with the need to think before making an action decision. In the decision-making process typical of human beings, which goes from data to "information", then from "information" to "knowledge" and finally from "knowledge" to "action decision", business experience should help to enrich and interpret predictions. Would it not be dangerous for our civilization to blindly rely on algorithms' predictions by forgetting the "knowledge" box, without trying to understand?

The situation is different in terms of pattern recognition due to deep learning. In this case, even if it is not yet possible to explain mathematically "why it works", it is possible to let the algorithm go directly to the result. The comparison between prediction and reality, carried out in prior studies, showed the strength and validity of the method. However, in insurance, concerning prices and provisions, the truth of the facts will come too late to correct an accumulation of prediction errors uncorrected over time: the insurer risks not being able to meet their commitments. Moreover, the regulator will not allow it and will require that regular reporting, established according to proven methods, explain the decisions by interpretable modeling.

For insurance companies, the new data-driven methods thus enrich risk assessment and claims to enrich techniques, but they cannot replace them.

On the contrary, as with any other economic activity, the new data of big data and new techniques are a great opportunity, especially for marketing, client relations and management. By knowing clients better, they will help to build offers that are more adapted to new needs.

The predictive dimension of algorithms can also enable insurers to add value through a real accountability and prevention role, as they did in the 20th Century for road safety and industrial risks.

4.3.2. *Personalized marketing and refined prices*

Clients are demanding personalization and "fair prices". This demand is somewhat contradictory to the principle of mutualization of insurance: it is because, for a group of clients, each person pays a price agreed in advance, that everyone will be sure to be compensated if he/she is unlucky to have a claim. In order to establish their prices, insurers divide their clients into risk groups that are assumed to be "homogeneous", defined according to the statistics they have on the past and some simple criteria concerning clients or what is insured. It is obvious that, at the end of the insurance period (usually 1 year), some clients will have paid "for nothing" and others will have been compensated well beyond their contribution. By construction, insurance makes losers and winners.

Will the desire for personalization call this principle into question? Is it selfish individualism on the part of clients? It would be the profession itself that would be threatened. Unless mutualization is done differently, big data gives clients an opportunity to carry it out outside of regulated and capitalized insurance companies.

Clients' new demand is pushing some insurers towards finer price segmentation. In compliance with regulations and ethics, the digital traces left by clients can allow insurers to better do their job and refine price classes in the same way as the current price classes without disruption. However, is this understandable for clients? Does this correspond to their demands? It should be accompanied by appropriate marketing segmentation, which could be finer than price segmentation. It is through marketing and communication with clients that insurers will be able to make a difference. In this improvement process that is not really disruptive, it is marketing segmentation that makes it possible to meet demand, and there, data contribution is essential for the insurer, as for all companies. Because marketing segmentation does not have to be justified in any way other than by its efficiency, it can benefit from all innovation possibilities brought by machine learning, by the contribution of external data – particularly with open data, data-driven learning, and even "black box" algorithms. Insurers can push the offers to the right client segments with the right arguments and the right associated services, without prices being different.

Client data make it possible to follow their moments of life and to anticipate their needs (change of car or housing upon the birth of a child, for example). This enables them to be profiled for a specific purpose (always in compliance with regulations) and to better understand the type of relationship and services they want. For example, do they like receiving information alerts or advice on their smartphone or not?

For clients who accept, a connected relationship via a bracelet or home automation objects for example, it can lead to reductions in prices or gifts, in a spirit of prevention as a reward for virtuous behavior.

These practices have the disadvantage of being normative and not always based on scientifically relevant criteria. Why should one walk 10,000 steps a day? Why not 9,000 or 12,000? And if I only walk 5,000 steps a day, but I swim 10 laps, am I not a "good" risk?

In effect, are these changes, which are based on client relationship and not prices, sufficient to meet expectations?

We see ideas of price differentiation emerging here and there, pushed to extremes that would undermine the current economic model and would probably lead to unbearable prices for some clients, thus excluding them from the insurance system, with serious consequences for the community.

Market dynamics would change the portfolios in a way that is difficult to predict since it involves multi-actor games. An insurer implementing very low prices for the supposed "good" risks and high prices for the supposed "bad" risks, may lose a good part of their portfolio and unbalance their accounts by a decrease in revenue that has not been netted because their staff, management and premises' fixed costs are being contained.

The overall solvency of the insurance market could be undermined by such practices.

Moreover, a refining of prices, which could go as far as individualization, would have another "perverse" technical effect. It is clear that the finer the segmentation, the more likely the insurer may be mistaken in the evaluation of their commitments. The insurer is obliged to take a wider safety margin and therefore to globally implement technical prices higher than what is necessary and with a larger pooling.

In this situation, the regulation and regulator require a higher capitalization, which calls for a return on capital. An extremely refined segmentation would require a greater mobilization of capital, which could be costly and would therefore generally run counter to collective interest.

A balance must therefore be found in the level of mutualization of insurance to take into account the acceptability of the solidarity dimension contained in the current pooling and to meet the aspirations of a portion of clients for the personalization of prices.

4.3.3. *New offers based on new criteria*

Another way of meeting the demand for individualization is to link the insurance price directly to an objective index of the insured risk or behavior of the client that is supposed to account for this risk level.

New insurance criteria thus emerged: in car insurance, for example, where the motorist's driving behavior is "scored" according to parameters such as braking, acceleration, pace, change of direction, geolocation and driving times, a calibration is necessary with the usual pricing methods.

In the new digital world, one does not wait to know everything to act. We learn by acting: test and learn. The approach is inference. It is the data that dictate the trajectory, which is permanently rectified according to each acquisition of relevant information. Even though portfolio monitoring requires that all instants are actuarially sound, actuarial bases are not called into question.

Big data and open data are also very useful for the development of parametric insurance such as storm insurance whose prior agreed indemnity is triggered solely on the basis of a wind index, regardless of any possible damage caused. Mixed insurance, partly parametric and partly compensational, is also envisaged, particularly in agricultural insurance. Beyond weather data, insurers can use drones and satellites to measure the field's dryness or grass height.

Numerous one-time card insurances can also be found. Offers can be available on mobile devices in applications, but can also be "shifted" to smartphones, thanks to geolocation, for clients who want it (while being very attentive to regulations). There are many opportunities: insurance to be underwritten just before borrowing a vehicle from a friend, or before skiing, etc.

In these situations, similar to those of organizations that grant credits related to the purchase of objects, machine learning and big data are essential because prices must be made as quickly as possible. Pricing is of course difficult and actuarial monitoring is arduous, but for small sums, the technical safety margin can no doubt be found.

Therefore, a vast field of possibilities is open to insurers, marketers and actuaries who will have a creative freedom. It will be necessary to ensure that claims occurrence is in line with risk assessments and it will also be important to measure whether the additional cost of using these technologies will be well-compensated by the gains in underwriting and disaster expertise.

4.3.4. *New risks to be insured*

Any new technology has its setbacks. In view of the tremendous opportunities of digital and big data, a quite impressive piracy industry is developing, which profits from everything-connected.

IT security has become an ongoing concern of the DIS, as all companies are hacked and often repeatedly, and individuals are demanded ransoms for their PC data to be restored after attack. In 2015, according to the Global Economic Crime Survey – PwC, cybercrime cost French companies 3.36 billion euros. Frauds affecting the president, phishing, data theft, individuals, by their naivety or negligence as regards cyber risks, are the vectors of the success of cyber attacks in half of the cases. Connected objects are the other weak link in the devices. They are not properly secured when designed, are not subject to maintenance and are a preferred entry point for hackers.

There is a great need for companies to cover these new risks. Not only are their data essential to the exercise of their business, but any loss of data presents corporate image risks and loss of confidence. In this respect, as regards personal data, the new European regulation (entry into force and mandatory application in May 2018) tightens the requirements: it provides for very severe financial sanctions in case of data theft if all security measures have not been taken.

Cyber security insurance is essential to the new economic world. It constitutes a new market requiring strong growth, for which much is to be constructed. This field of development falls within the context of data privacy, which makes risk assessment very difficult. Data scarcity requires new suitable modeling, which needs research in actuarial mathematics.

The generalization of algorithms and robotization perspective of many intellectual tasks open a new field of insurance needs. How to secure them depends on the legal framework that will be set for robots. The European Parliament is currently working on this subject, and for the time being, the creation of a specific status for robots is being rejected, which makes it possible to remain within the current insurance framework.

It is likely that accidents that will occur with autonomous cars will require adjustments in the current contracts. There is also the probability that pedestrians' behavior as well as that of other users of the public space will be modified by taking the robots' rationality into account. Will pedestrians, now in a state of inferiority compared to cars, change their behavior? Is it sure that autonomous cars will be programmed to let them pass, will they be very daring and cross the streets anyhow?

Risk assessment will therefore be different, but the need for coverage will not be eliminated. Autonomous cars will not escape certain classical disasters and will also generate new risks, including cyber threats.

4.3.5. *New methods to better serve and manage clients*

Big data and the exploitation of heterogeneous data (emails, telephone exchanges, email complaints, amicable declarations, site visits, satellite images, etc.) are valuable sources for improving management, reducing time and cost as well as for data quality.

A faster sorting of claims files, providing better service for clients including a more accurate evaluation of provisions, detection of attrition, anticipation, fraud deterrence and detection, improvement and harmonization of databases, are all enormous works to be properly carried out in order to serve and retain clients by way of safe, efficient and economical management.

To make the reality of this big data world more perceptible, data visualization techniques help to visualize results in a synthetic, but also dynamic and multifaceted way, by making them move according to certain parameters: time, place, etc.

These techniques are of great help insofar as they do not give rise to a skillful presentation that comes close to the point of manipulation.

4.4. Risks weakening of the business: competition from new actors, "uberization", contraction of market volume

Although big data revolution places insurers at risk, it also generates many fantasies.

4.4.1. *The risk of demutualization*

The first risk mainly depends on the insurers themselves: these are the risks of demutualization and exclusion of certain policyholders. If some major insurers engage in extreme hyper-segmentation, with price reductions as the key to ensuring "good risks", they are likely to initially achieve commercial success. It will be difficult for other insurers to resist this trend, especially as the possibly poor financial results will not be immediately apparent. It should be borne in mind that the detection of "good risks" is not as easy as it seems and that technical balances are a real business, well-controlled by existing insurers with traditional techniques.

However, once the dynamism is triggered, the market would be permanently destabilized and remedying the situation would become problematic. Will the ACPR protect the market from such a drift? This is for the safety of all. The exclusion of policyholders who are considered to be "bad risks", who would be offered only prohibitive high prices in the absence of solidarity, would put the community at risk.

The same is true for the overall solvency of the market and durability of the insurance business. It is the sustainability of these major financial market investors, needed to finance debt and the economy, that is at stake.

Without going as far as this extreme hypothesis, we must remember that hyper-segmentation mechanically increases the uncertainty on insurance companies' results, hence the capital requirements to ensure solvency, and in turn increasing the cost for insurers and therefore prices.

4.4.2. *The risk of "uberization"*

The economic model of digital platforms has demonstrated its effectiveness and destructive impact on existing actors.

GAFA (Google, Apple, Facebook and Amazon), and especially NATU (Netflix, Airbnb, Tesla and Uber), are experiencing tremendous growth at the expense of existing companies: hotel groups, central taxi services, etc.; in 2016, Airbnb's sales increased by 80%, and Uber by 267%. Traditional models are hampered by these digital, agile newcomers, with little or no employees, with no hardware assets other than computers, which give access to higher-quality and cheaper services, by interposing between businesses and their clients without taking the risks of these businesses but by taking a large part of the financial margin.

After bookshops, restaurants, hotels, taxis, etc., will insurers fall victim to digital platforms and let them cut them off from their traditional clients and distributors? Will they be intermediated, become technical and management subcontractors, carry all the risks in their balance sheets, but lose their clients, strategic latitude and part of their profitability?

In some way, the multiplicity of insurance distribution channels (employees, agents, brokers, IAM), which complicates the digitization of insurers but roots client relationship in physical networks, has the advantage of making it more difficult for a possible predator "platform" to take power.

4.4.3. *The risk of an omniscient "Google" in the dominant position due to data*

The most feared potential competitor would be Google or another major digital actor having a large amount of fine data on clients and their privacy.

Indeed, the specificity of the reverse cycle of insurance requires that, in order to be effective, a new insurer should offer more attractive prices and be able to direct its offerings to the appropriate client segments. This requires that it has the information (and skills) to identify "good risks". In this respect, GAFA and NATU are ideally placed: they know more about insurers' clients than the insurers themselves.

It is true that, thanks to all the information we give them about us without being aware of it, they know everything about us. But is that enough to assess the risk? Is it really that easy to detect "good risks?" And what is a good risk? Is the insurer's profession so simple? Is behavior enough to prevent the future? Is life "just?"

After several small trials in France and Great Britain in particular, as a broker, Google has not (yet?) launched an attack.

4.4.4. *The risk of competition with new companies created for a digital world*

One of the difficulties of traditional insurance companies lies in digital transformation. The issue is to make the complexity of managing the multitude of existing contracts, which are very diverse and not designed for the digital world, compatible with the new requirements of client experience.

If the insurance business did not require strong capitalization and proven expertise (such as the ability to convince the ACPR to issue an authorization), it is likely that several new companies would have been created on new technological bases with products, customer communication methods and an information system perfectly adapted to big data context.

The strengthening of regulations aimed at enhancing data security and the privacy of policyholders is also moving in the direction of benefiting new insurance companies.

For example, the principle of privacy by design, which is one of the guiding principles of the GDPR (General Data Protection Regulation), is not favorable to well-established insurance companies whose portfolios have accumulated several generations of contracts for more than half a century. The legal dimension and reverse cycle of insurance business solidify the commitments made and the products that support them. It is not easy to move clients from a former contract to a new one because of the commercial and management costs involved and the risk of losing the client's incentive to reopen the contract.

Similarly, the newfound obligation for companies to provide clients with all the data held on them is easy for a new company, but this is difficult for an "old" company whose large databases were structured in a completely different context.

In fact, the entry barrier is high. As proof, so far, only one new digital company, Alan, was created in October 2016 to cover health, the primary target being the clients of start-ups.

4.4.5. *The risk of reduction in the scope of property insurance*

Societal evolutions are changing consumption habits.

Is preference for usage at the expense of property a basic tendency or a temporary consequence of the economic crisis? If it persists, it profoundly alters several important branches of property insurance, including car insurance. The development of usage shifts "damage" risk from individuals to companies (renters, manufacturers, etc.) and can considerably reduce the volume, since companies have a high self-insurance capacity, especially when they are well placed for maintenance and repair.

This risk of shift from B2C to B2B is increased by the emergence of wholesale brokers under a collaborative economy (peer-to-peer) who design new offerings adapted for the digital world, for organized communities; aiming at lower prices and better service. Inspeer, Otherwise and Wecover are good French examples.

This reduces the insured volume because communities have a more comfortable financial base than an individual and can assume higher deductibles.

Some are relevant regarding accountability and prevention which justifies lower prices.

The insurer's profit margin can be retained, but the turnover may be threatened. This will require adjusting the size of the commercial and management mechanisms.

The recent media success of blockchain technology releases creativity and opens up many opportunities, including some fantasies. Some envisage a mutualization between individuals, outside of any insurance company, within a blockchain: in the United States, Teamumbrella, for example, manages automobile risk in a "community" without a legal structure, outside prudential regulation, which exposes them to insufficient resources to cover large claims.

Others go further and come out of any mutualization: they consider insurance a bet between two individuals. A bet for the "insured" individual who will not have recourse in the event of a serious disaster if the partner is insolvent in due course. And a bet for the partner if the amount of the loss is greater than expected. Betting preset amounts would not solve the problems.

4.4.6. *The risk of non-access to data or prohibition of use*

In today's big data world, for insurers, access to the data of policyholders is not as natural as it seems. In the case of distribution by brokers, the client is that of the broker and not of the insurer. Multichannel distribution complicates organization. As policyholders are increasingly mobile, one policyholder can be client of the insurer by underwriting with an employee of the insurer or, for another risk, client of a broker. It is difficult for the insurer to consolidate all this information: data governance is an issue of real importance.

Moreover, regulatory changes, which aim at protecting consumers, fall in line with a restriction of the choice of pricing criteria, notably for non-discriminatory reasons. The European ban on the use of gender, which is nevertheless discriminatory for certain risks, is a glaring example.

The right to oblivion, for the benefit of patients who have suffered from certain serious illnesses, came into force in mid-February 2017. In order to underwrite a credit insurance contract, persons who suffered from cancer, without relapse for 5 years, are no longer required to declare their former disease.

In addition, the law provides for a reference grid that defines, by pathology, the periods within which people can underwrite an insurance without premium or disclaimer of warranty (AERAS). The ACPR ensures compliance with this right to oblivion.

Here, we notice contradictory wishes: on the one hand, the authorities' concern to ensure the protection of individuals' privacy and combat discrimination, a precaution to which the public adheres; on the other hand, the wish of individuals to be treated within their particularism and benefit from personalized offers. This does not facilitate insurers' tasks, especially as the client experience of other economic activities, based on tangible products, is not hampered by the same measures and controls on the use of data.

4.4.7. *The risk of cyber attacks and the risk of non-compliance*

Like any technological revolution, big data and algorithms can generate the best and the worst. If digital "increases" insurers and clients, criminals also increase. And since the law does not move as fast as technology, hackers and criminals constantly take advantage of the power of data and algorithms.

The explosion of the number of connected objects, which constitute "computers" (even the most modest, like light bulbs), multiplies the risks of attacks. Connected objects are not very secure when designed and especially do not benefit from security maintenance. They are really the weak links in the digital world.

Companies are bound by security obligations that are an obstacle to their creativity. Not only do they have to comply with the law, which is normal, it is equally up to them to prove their compliance. In this respect, the new European GDPR is very demanding: companies have to take the blame if, victim of data theft, they cannot prove that they had taken all the necessary security measures, including their subcontractors. Established sanctions are very heavy (up to 4% of global turnover) and can lead companies to bankruptcy.

As consumers, we all enjoy this protection. However, our security is threatened by hackers who do not hesitate to deploy their creativity to steal and hold insurers' data for ransom.

This situation poses a double risk to insurers: the risk of not being able to ensure compliance and that of not countering all hackers' attacks. Their reputation and the confidence that clients place in them depend on doing something about it.

4.4.8. *Risks of internal rigidities and training efforts to implement*

Finally, one of the main risks lies in the difficulty of successfully achieving internal digital transformation. It is not just about making the right technical decisions at the top of the company and having highly specialized data specialists. It is the entire company that has to take ownership of the new digital world.

It is necessary to move the entire organization towards more agility, with test and learn experiments and the right to make mistakes, with more internal transversal and collaborative working, including cooperations with partners: start-ups for example, as well as wholesale brokers and even co-construction with clients.

This requires a major effort with regard to staff training and profound changes in management trends.

4.5. Ethical and trust issues

In the reverse cycle economic model of insurance, client trust is fundamental. It is obviously based on the insurer's solvency, their full respect of the confidentiality of data, as well as the quality of their reputation. Regarding client data, the insurance principle has always been based on trust: clients provide the insurer with sincere information about their situation, thus enabling the insurer to evaluate their commitment and propose a contract. The insurer promises to keep the collected information confidential.

This asymmetry of information is called into question by the digital world. On the one hand, in some cases the digital world changes the asymmetry and gives advantage to the client. The genome is a good example since clients will soon be able to use it for a small fee, whereas the insurer will not know the predictions it contains and in any case would not have the right to use the information. On the other hand, via connected objects such as bracelets or cars, the insurer directly collects data without a need for the client's validation. The insurer assumes a share of responsibility regarding the relevance of the data they use to assess risk and set the price.

In the new digital world, the basis of trust between the client and the insurer are therefore modified in a number of cases.

Moreover, in the age of social networks, a grain of sand can destroy an image, any incident can be greatly amplified and everyone can be informed within minutes. Insurance companies are very attentive to this risk.

4.5.1. *Ethical charter and labeling: proof of loyalty*

There are many dangers, including cyber attacks, which insurers may experience despite all their efforts.

However, through the insurer's ethics and way of getting employees to adhere, dangers can be limited. By neglecting these precautions, they may put themselves in a situation of failing as regards the loyalty they owe to their clients, with disastrous consequences on their reputation should this be revealed. This requires a special effort, because, if we are not careful, big data and algorithms can lead to such failure.

Indeed, beyond the responsibility of some employees whose naivety and negligence facilitate the intrusion of hackers into systems, big data and machine learning algorithms generate in themselves risks to the protection of people's privacy. Big data leads individuals to provide platforms with all sorts of behavioral information that is often insignificant and which, processed by the power of machine learning, makes it possible to unwittingly attribute a profile to them, in a legal way, without needing to know their identity.

This has the following advantages: better informed about clients, the insurer can give them better advice, offer them a contract more suited to their needs and a more refined price. However, this can also lead to re-identifications and discriminatory practices.

Even if regulations (CNIL law, European GDPR, Lemaire law) are working to protect individuals, the right is struggling to capture digital technology. This is why the legislator does not precisely define what is authorized, but lays down guiding principles. These principles are decisive: the principle of privacy by design so that all precautions are taken for the confidentiality of client data from product design, as well as the principle of accountability that empowers the company and gives the regulator the freedom to appreciate *ex post* if there has been a fault, and the principle of loyalty whose application is very difficult to prove objectively.

For insurers, it is this loyalty that must convince clients. There is a relationship of trust. Convincing is a difficult task. It is not enough to announce one's good intentions: it is necessary to be able to show the measures taken to implement them and, if possible, to make their effectiveness validated by an independent third party.

Insurers can be assisted by the establishment of an ethical charter, a commitment relating to the training of their staff testifying the resources mobilized and the precautions taken, by total transparency with regard to clients concerning data held on them. Many insurers have taken this direction.

They may also have a third party to testify the precautions taken: labeling of their processes or even their algorithms, choice of algorithms that ban "black boxes" and allowing the interpretability of results.

This requires ethical training of the teams so that, from the design of algorithms and throughout the processing chain, each employee is attentive to loyalty as regards clients: strictly respecting the regulations on data (personal, sensitive, health), using information classification CIA (confidentiality, availability, integrity and proof) criteria, without introducing cultural bias that may lead to discrimination, using data adapted to the purpose in a parsimonious way.

It is also necessary to formalize the Chinese walls between organizations authorized to process personal data in compliance with regulations (purpose of processing, informed consent of the client, etc.) and insurers. They can, for example, work from scores without access to personal data.

It is essential to be careful about the quality of the data used. For example, are the data provided by connected bracelets reliable? Taking personalized pricing decisions, based on inaccurate data, may be very counterproductive to an insurer and damaging to their reputation. Wrong personalization is in general more hard-felt than a standard price.

4.5.2. *Price, ethics and trust*

Big data makes some economic actors, such as SNCF, airlines or hoteliers, practice yield management, a pricing management system for available capacities, which aims at optimizing filling and turnover. This leads them to price differentiations, which correspond to their own financial interest at a given moment, in line with their marginal economic balance sheet at that moment, rather than the average cost for all their clients or even homogeneous segments of clients (same periods or schedules). They thus practice extremely different prices for the same service, according to their criteria, which are often not related to clients.

Some of these actors go further and use the information they have on clients to increase the prices of those who can afford it. This practice, carried out without transparency, raises ethical questions. For insurers, it would be technically possible to practice yield management, for example, by differentiating prices from online subscriptions based on the profiles of clients already in the portfolio in order to distribute and balance the risks.

How would this practice, accepted for trains, planes and hotel rooms, be welcomed by clients if insurers offered it to them? Because what clients are asking their insurers for today are "fair prices". This requirement seems far removed from the practice of yield management.

But what is a "fair price?" Would price differentiation made without the knowledge of clients on the basis of their wealth (detected thanks to these data) not appear "fair" to some less affluent clients? Is this "technical correctness" (cost of service)? Or "justness" in the sense of "value of service rendered?" Or "moral justice?"

The imprecise nature of the current demand for personalization, which runs counter to mutualization, which is the basis of insurance, is in fact an embarrassing unknown in defining the insurer's strategy. What pricing ethics do consumers expect from their insurers? To what extent is the insurer constrained in their ability to innovate prices by the unformulated expectations of their clients? How can trust be strengthened or on the contrary undermined? Do insurers have to hold on to their mutualization base or abandon themselves to the digital marketing trend that flatters consumers in the short term? Should insurance become a consumer good like any other? Follow the fashion? Or, on the contrary, preserve an image of "institution" not really fun, but solid, protective and lasting.

This should not prevent insurers from taking advantage of big data to obtain the value of data, modernize its products and services, lower management and fraud costs, listen to clients, keep up with changing needs, adapt and even anticipate them.

4.6. Mobilization of insurers in view of big data

As early as 2011, MetLife, a long-established insurance company (149 years in 2017), was the first insurer to embark on big data. A leading life insurance company in the United States, present in 60 countries, within 3 months, thanks to its big data project "The Wall", which implemented an all-channel synthetic and unique "360° client view", breaking the boundaries between the "business" silots, which is standard among all insurers. This project, which had been included in the strategic plan for several years, was not implemented due to the lack of suitable technologies, until big data made it possible with a Facebook approach.

In France, it was in 2013 and especially in 2014 that insurers took the arrival of this third industrial revolution very seriously. However, at the time big data was still considered by some as a fashion phenomenon. Other insurers were, in contrast, quite concerned, fearing the upcoming competition from an "insurance free", Google or other GAFA, whose financial strength and masses of data could come and "uberize" existing insurers.

4.6.1. *A first-phase "new converts"*

First, the impetus was given by the Directorates-General and quite substantial budgets were granted for the hiring of eminent data scientists and marketers of the distribution sector, supported by communication. Data lakes, Hadoop computer architectures and datalabs were mounted, and chief data officers were appointed.

Actuaries mobilized to acquire the new skills needed in data science (Python code language, random forest algorithms, etc.) in addition to their traditional skills, to exploit all types of data. A training exercise on data science for actuarial purposes was set up by the Institute of Actuaries for active actuaries. Despite the significant mobilization of actuarial means required by the implementation of Solvency II, existing professionals began to invest in the digital field.

To disseminate digital culture in all the teams, chief digital officers were appointed to promote the necessary digital evolution, foster cross-functionalities and recognize creativity and initiative. Despite the digital days and other events intended for company employees, digital penetration in the entire processing chain has often proved difficult. It must be noted that it is very difficult to carry out the tasks of existing activities, complicated by the profound changes in regulations, and the efforts needed for digital transformation.

The first orientations mainly concerned marketing, following the example of companies in the consumer and telephony sector. KYC (Know Your Customer), which has become known as "client experience" and client knowledge, was at the center of the action.

However, from 2015, some were interested in the benefits of obtaining data for management. BNP Paribas Cardif, for example, launched the "Kaggle" competition in that respect (international competition of algorithms based on real anonymized data).

In the study services, a lot of work was being done to try to take advantage of the data, notably weather data, geolocation data and more generally data of open data to enrich the internal data. A large number of actuarial papers were thus submitted in order to get required diplomas. Many POCs (proofs of concept) have been developed in marketing and actuarial services, the new order inducing the two professions to cooperate in multi-skills teams, instead of working sequentially as usual.

A certain confidentiality surrounds this work. It is difficult to know the exact level of progress of insurance companies. However, it appears that, to date, few of these prototypes have been transformed into products or services. One of the explanations often put forward is the difficulty of integrating these innovations into existing processes.

4.6.2. *A phase of appropriation and experimentation in different fields*

Big data gives rise to entrepreneurship: many young Assurtechs are created, full of enthusiasm and new ideas. This movement is particularly noticeable in insurance: while the amount of capital invested in Fintech decreases in finances, it has been multiplied by 20 in 5 years for Assurtech in insurance (source: CB *Insights*).

Insurers have a great interest in the activity of these young fledgling entrepreneurs and their capacity for disruptive innovation. They support them in various ways: incubators, partnerships, equity investments, etc. Some are trying to integrate them to revitalize their organizations; others prefer to leave them aside so as to avoid polluting their creativity by being too close to everyday constraints. Some invest in equity; others provide resources or participate alongside them with the Unique Interministerial Fund (projects financed by the State through competitiveness clusters).

The input of external data is often done with the help of specialized start-ups.

Thus, Covea, in collaboration with BlueDME, has launched a platform giving access to thousands of external data, with a recommendation engine, making it easier for its employees to search for relevant datasets for a given purpose.

In fact, big data is not henceforth confined to data lab data scientists' teams. The digital world is gradually progressing at the heart of companies, often with minor adjustments, in different sectors.

In the actuarial field, it already helps in improving and accelerating the calculation of provisions. Disaster management is better organized and accelerated by sorting files using text data or other heterogeneous data, but much remains to be done as artificial intelligence progresses. The assessment of severe claims is subject to processing by algorithms with data enriched by external data and their assessment is refined. This allows for better provisioning and less capital requirements.

Thus, improving management has several advantages: management costs are lowered and provisioning amounts are adjusted. This tends to reduce capital requirements and clients are compensated faster. In the future, will it be possible to go as far as advanced robotization of claims management, as recently experienced in Japan, where a company will replace 34 employees (25%) from one of its services by artificial intelligence (Watson explorer)?

The refinement of prices is a significant study topic for actuaries, but not necessarily focused on a lower level of mutualization.

One of the key issues for insurers is combating attrition: it is an important issue for profitability because it costs a lot more trying to win a new client than striving to develop client loyalty as regards those in the portfolio.

In life insurance, the prediction of total and partial redemptions is also improved by big data, in particular by knowing the clients' moments of life.

Another important area of application of big data, a source of substantial savings, is the fight against fraud. The FFA (French Federation of Insurance) and its Alpha structure have been entirely working on this since 2014, with the start-up Shift Technology. Some market actors use the IBM Watson system. Watson has set up a real-time operational anti-fraud platform in the optical and dental sector for ProBTP: Solon. It aims at deterring, detecting and preventing fraud.

To improve the relationship with clients, some initiatives are aimed at giving them the keys to the legal language of insurance contracts, often considered by individuals as jargon intended to confuse policyholders. Thus, Aviva utilise Alexa, the intelligent assistant of Amazon, to make the insurance vocabulary readable.

Simplifying and streamlining client relationships in real time is a constant concern for insurance companies.

Since the smartphone has become the preferred tool of consumers for their purchases, great efforts are being made to develop applications for mobiles. Prevention alerts are sent to clients to inform them of the risks of storms, for example.

Like MetLife, the "360°" client vision is an objective for insurers. In this regard, MMA (Marketing Management Analytics), for example, deployed in 2016 a tool enabling client relationship actors to easily access a client's entire data when establishing contact.

Another area of development concerns assistance to compliance with regulations. A wave of innovations comes from Asia with start-ups (called Regtech) that propose solutions to facilitate the management of insurers' constraints and client knowledge (KYC).

Other actors focus on facilitating the financial management of their clients' savings. SwissLife, a major life insurer, cautious about new technologies, nevertheless invested in Budget Insight's Fin Box API, an application that gives individuals a global vision of their financial assets, in order to encourage the activity of its team of 800 specialists in wealth management. Wealth management consultancy is also a privileged area for the use of big data and AI (artificial intelligence). Robo-advisors, offering asset allocations and automated management, can bring services that are equivalent to those of WMC (Wealth Management Consultants) within everyone's reach, without human intervention. They are very successful in Asia and are beginning to appear in France.

Artificial intelligence is also introduced in distribution through recommendation tools provided to account managers. Crédit Mutuel called in Watson to equip its network, with account managers retaining some flexibility with regard to adjustments and decisions.

Chatbots (conversational robots) are emerging, following Facebook Messenger and successful experiments in other sectors: Voyages SNCF, PMU (Pari Mutuel Urban), Accor Hotels, Meetic, Air France KLM, etc. These conversational robots, which are available 24 h a day, 7 days a week, have the huge advantage of improving client experience while eventually opening the way to lower costs. Bots are still quite rudimentary and cannot manage clients' path from A to Z. But with the stunning progress of NLP (natural language processing in Neuro-Linguistic Programming), it seems quite probable that these bots are going to generalize and indeed replace applications.

4.6.3. *Changes in organization and management and major training efforts to be carried out*

Such changes of trades have a direct impact on employees. Certainly, the example must come from above. We must invent new management methods and be more collective and more inclusive. In this regard, Thomas Bubbler, CEO of the AXA group, expresses insurers' state of mind: "limiting innovation to technology would be a mistake because it must permeate our entire corporate culture [...] At the highest level of the company, one of my first decisions was to change the way top management meets, to create new spaces for dialogue and make senior executives real partners."

The HRDs of insurance companies are mobilized to make the teams evolve towards a more transversal and collaborative mode of work and for the training of staff on new aspects of digital technology: training on digital techniques internally, external training that will possibly lead to a qualification, to acquire skills in R coding or Python, or in computer architecture, or mathematical algorithms, as well as training required for compliance.

The training must also cover compliance with the new regulations on personal data and the protection of privacy. In general, charters have been put in place at the corporate or skilled trade level, such as, for actuaries who are members of the Institute of Actuaries who must ensure compliance with the code of ethics.

It is also the responsibility of HRDs, in collaboration with CIOs and managers, to disseminate a culture of computer security. Cyber attacks are very often facilitated by the naivety and ignorance of employees who fall into traps set by hackers. Good training would greatly limit these risks, which are among the most significant operational risks for insurance companies.

4.6.4. *A new form of insurance: "connected" insurance*

The great disruption of insurance offerings, often announced, is still a long way off. For the moment, the impact of digital technology has little to do with the core of the insurance business and its actuarial basis for mutualization.

The area in which developments are most evident is that of insurance through connected objects (IoT): it seems to be the way of future contracts innovation. Many insurers have entered into partnerships with manufacturers of connected objects, the idea being, in particular, to create a close relationship with clients and not to be cut off from this contact by manufacturers of connected objects that are at the source of the data.

Struggles and strategic collaborations are currently taking place at this level between insurers, car manufacturers, telephony operators, etc.

Different tele-assistance offers intended for home care of the elderly have been launched: Groupama, Harmonie Mutuelle, Mondial Assistance, Allianz and AXA. However, for now, they are all complaining that this market is not taking off.

According to a study conducted by Accenture in 2015 in several countries, out of 400 insurance companies, 50% see in this new type of insurance a new source of income in the years to come, of which 40% have already launched at least one offer based on a connected object. The scope of application, limited initially to car insurance and to a certain lifestyle (connected bracelets), extends to houses and company buildings, prevention as well as health. In France, the rate of insurers having launched an offer based on IoT is only 26%, which can be explained by the situation of the French market: car insurance with classical contracts is cheaper in France than in other countries, leaving less margin for pricing advantages to be granted to "good risks" for behavior-based insurance.

As for health insurance, the scope of insurers is much more limited than in other countries because of the importance of social security, and the culture that prevails in France in this area makes clients suspicious of insurers.

As regards car insurance, Allianz and AXA have created offers whose pricing depends on driving behavior: pay how you drive. Acceleration or sudden braking, excessively sharp turns and a too fast pace, marked by connected vehicle data, are not good indicators and should be avoided in order to obtain price reductions.

These new offerings certainly attract some interest, but to date, they have not resulted in massive cancellations of classical contracts, while the pricing advantage is not small for "good" drivers: AXA Global Direct promises a reduction of up to 50%. This advantage probably creates a bias in the recruitment of good drivers because, according to the company, the average rate of reduction would be 21% in 2017. The portfolio and its actuarial balance is monitored on a daily basis and the individualization of contributions is approached with caution.

The fairly moderate level of success to date regarding these offerings may also be explained by the reluctance of consumers to submit their data to their insurer. Insurers take care, however, to make parsimonious use of the data and only access those that are useful to them. At Allianz, for example, geolocation is only accessible in the event of an accident.

This fear of misuse by the insurer strongly emerged when Generali announced the launch of its Vitality offer in France. This is a complementary health offer, which gives gifts in the form of advantages to the insurer's partners (Decathlon, Fnac, Club Med, etc.) to persons who commit to a lifestyle program, monitored by balance or connected bracelet, corresponding to their personal situation, which is established from an online questionnaire. The offer is included in a collective contract, underwritten by a company, in which employees are protected by regulations: the price must be the same for all the underwriter's employees and any exclusion is prohibited.

Within the insurance contract, adherence to the Vitality program is not compulsory. For employees who have joined the program, the data are collected and processed by an external body. The employer and insurer only have access to a score calculated by the body; the employee is guaranteed that this score will be used for nothing other than this Vitality program.

However, all these guarantees do not seem to fully reassure clients. It seems indeed that in France, clients, already a little reluctant to communicate their data to car insurers, are even more reluctant when it comes to health insurers.

However, according to a study conducted by Accenture, this situation could change: at the global level, 67% of people surveyed are willing to pass on personal data to their banks or wealth management companies in order to benefit from better services. This rate drops to 57% for insurance contracts. The same observation is recorded outside of France. For banking services, 59% of French people may submit personal data. For an insurance contract, they are, however, fewer in number (49%). However, for valuable advice on financial investments, they are 64%.

The tendency for the provision of data in return for advantages is expected to increase in the future as the younger generation differs from that of its elders by a very different attitude. Not only are young people addicted to digital offers, but for them, traditional insurers are not their privileged interlocutors. Their priority is speed and ease of access; they do not project into the future, do not really trust promises and are not sure of the protection that institutions can offer them. "Our future competitors are Amazon, Apple or Facebook," Thomas Buberl, Chief Executive Officer of AXA Group, told Echos in 2017.

4.6.5. *Insurtech and collaborative economy press for innovation*

From the first breakthroughs of collaborative economy in the area of mobility, insurers positioned themselves to accompany the start-ups that support them: car-pooling (BlaBlaCar, TravelCar) and private rental types such as OuiCar have entered into partnerships with insurers.

However, real insurance offer innovations appeared recently in the context of collaborative economy, under the pressure of young Assurtechs. InsPeer, Otherwise and WeCover worked to establish suitable offers to communities. The techniques and offers are different but the general idea of these offers is almost the same: bringing to the insurer groups of clients who wish to pool their risks. These groups cover a first level of claims and subscribe to contracts beyond a high deductible amount. The common interest of group members is to adopt reasonable behavior, which tends to reduce claims. The coverage guaranteed by insurers is lower than those with individual subscriptions, but on the one hand, they are spared small-scale claims, which reduce their management costs, and on the other hand, the community is supposed to put a virtuous pressure on its members that would normally reduce claims.

These start-ups usually operate as a brokerage firm: Otherwise's solutions are underpinned by several insurers, including Thélem; the insurance company Suravenir Assurances will carry contracts designed by WeCover in its balance sheet.

Co-construction is a new area of development that falls within the context of collaborative societal evolution and is based on collective intelligence.

Reaching out to the client community to co-create, gather opinions and design future products and services is an ongoing trend. Many insurers, such as AXA, Covea and BNP Paribas Cardif, also work in partnership with prestigious universities, sometimes within the framework of Research Chairs.

4.7. Strategy avenues for the future

Big data left insurers with the fear of a head-on entry into the market of a major competitor like Google, which, knowing all the clients, could greatly attract the "good" clients with attractive prices and marginalize existing insurers in difficult and unprofitable sub-markets.

Google has made several attempts to enter the market in France and Britain, notably as a broker, but, for the moment, has given up on pursuing this path.

If it occurs, the disruption will likely take another form.

Big data, algorithms and progress in artificial intelligence are changing the world dramatically. The third industrial revolution, which is underway, makes any projection in the future very difficult: the strategic risk is increasing.

4.7.1. *Paradoxes and anticipation difficulties*

The current situation is paradoxical in many respects. Mass data and predictive algorithms provide prediction flows. However, it has never been so risky to predict what place insurance would have in the future, in a new world which today is greatly evolving, with new economic models for industries and services and new consumption habits.

Clients want to be treated for what they are, which requires knowing them individually, but they are reluctant to have their insurer use their data and even access such data.

On the one hand, they need security, which the legislator is striving to satisfy by increasingly reinforcing insurers' constraints; on the other hand, they overtly surrender their most intimate data to the platforms and engage without guarantee in more or less improvised communities.

Big data dumps masses of data, but the regulator tends to restrict the ability of insurers to use them, as is the case with the right to oblivion, which marks a setback in insurers' freedom to price according to costs.

The world of big data and artificial intelligence allows the emergence of solutions that can robotize many complex tasks and alleviate management costs. However, the more connected objects develop, the more the cyber risk increases, bringing with it a threat of disasters of considerable magnitude.

The old legal framework is not suited to the new world: the authorities and civil society are working to redefine rules in order to establish a new order in a society that has lost its benchmarks, particularly in the use of algorithms and data. However, this poorly defined environment poses a risk of heavy financial sanctions if insurers suffer from a personal data disaster even though they believe to have made every effort to protect their clients but failed on one point of the processing chain (for example, one of its subcontractors). On the one hand, the insurer must take its share in the added value brought by big data. On the other hand, they are retrained in their capacity for innovation by these uncertainties.

Technology is evolving very quickly and agility is becoming a quality essential to survival, while the management of portfolio contracts is mobilizing increasingly significant resources to meet the growing requirements of solvency, competition and data security regulations.

In this context, it is not easy for insurers, who are long-term actors, to define the right strategy for the future.

Of all the possible hypotheses for the evolution of society, what are the most probable? Should each insurer choose the most effective strategy in the most probable hypothesis or most robust strategy regardless of the future, which will leave it with more degrees of freedom and the ability to adapt?

4.7.2. *Several possible choices*

In the new context of collaborative economics and preference for usage, at the expense of property ownership, part of the insurance so far subscribed by private individuals in B2C should move to B2B (underwriting by companies). When a company makes its own property available to individuals, it does not need the same type of insurance as individuals. As regards damage to property, the company, which is often the manufacturer, can self-insure itself, at least in part: the size of its risk portfolio is sufficient to avoid pooling them with other actors. The insurable base would be severely contracted. The market would be much more concentrated than today and would probably eliminate small actors in the concerned insurance areas. The margin rate could be maintained, but the volume of business and staffing requirements would be greatly impacted.

The hypothesis of a generalization of the IoT seems plausible: future arrival of autonomous cars, acceleration of home automation, connected cities, hygiene and health prevention via connected objects. This is the opinion of some insurers such as AXA and Allianz: they believe the future market will largely pass through the IoT. One of the risks of this scenario for the insurer is to be cut off from the source of the information that is captured by the manufacturer of connected objects, thus to be cut off from the client relationship and eventually their freedom of action, especially for their products and for controlling the level of their margin. A parry could consist of forging partnerships or acquiring companies that manufacture connected objects. This strategy may also allow for cross-agreements in B2B2C in order to offer manufacturers' clients other insurance contracts than those linked to the connected object. Insurers are indeed working in this direction.

However, in this scenario, another consequence is feasible: the establishment of conglomerates dedicated to a given function, such as mobility, health or connected home. In this case, for insurers, the danger of being marginalized and cut off from clients is great. Extensive partnerships should be forged with large groups in order to become the main trusted third party of these conglomerates – connected home integrator or care coordinator, for example. This would prevent insurance being diluted in multi-service offerings. The economic weight of insurers would be strengthened by the power of all members of the conglomerate. In this case, there would be little room for only one actor per major function (mobility, home, etc.), as is the case for web platforms where the dynamics of economic models exclude less efficient and less powerful actors.

In this hypothesis regarding the impact of the generalization of IoT as in the one where it would not seem the most determinant, the hypothesis of a hyper-price segmentation is plausible if clients' demand for a real personalization of prices is strong. But how far can price segmentation go? At what degree of homogeneity of risk level should one stop in the price schedules? From a technical point of view, the smaller the size of the "homogeneous" group, the less reliable the risk probability law of this group. Uncontrolled competition in this sense could present serious risks of destabilization of the market and jeopardize its solvency. It would be difficult for many actors on the ground to resist the movement if one of the major insurers ventured into it. The actuarial balance could lose its bearings: it would be difficult to rebalance the situation in the event of poor results. Depending on their position, clients, company culture and the communication policy carried out to date, insurers would have more or less flexibility in choosing the fineness of their segmentation and price difference between segments. They could choose to stand out despite the pressure and take the risk of losing some clients by maintaining a comfortable mutualization. Or, they could follow the trend by substantially lowering the prices of those identified as "good" risks and significantly increasing others, with no consideration other than financial efficiency for their insurance company. This situation would present a real likelihood of exclusion of persons who have become uninsurable by an unbearable price level. The consequences would be far-reaching for the community, which would have to assume in one way or the other the cost of claims incurred by third-party victims. Moreover, in the long term, the benefits for policyholders would be limited by an inevitable overall price increase due to greater volatility of results requiring a higher solvency margin. Would the regulator intervene to limit price differences, as it did in the past for the young drivers' car insurance price?

Insurance is above all a demutualization activity: people gather around a trusted third party to address possible future risks. Marketing and advertising have often damaged the "collaborative" image of insurance and this is especially unfortunate at this time when collaborative economy is becoming a reality. Is forgetting this basis not detrimental to the cohesion of our society? Insurance plays a fundamental social and economic role in society by allowing everyone to act and take life-related risks with the guarantee of being rescued in the event of a problem. Over-personalization of prices would risk calling this essential function into question. But will insurers have a choice if a major actor engages in the path of hyper-segmentation and thus disrupts market mechanisms?

In effect, in this time of collaborative economy, another option would be possible for insurers: re-enchanting insurance by returning to the basics of the business and re-establishing mutualization on new bases. An avenue is provided by the current peer-to-peer trend, which encourages consumers to gather into pressure groups (petitions) or groups of buyers in order to generate spontaneous demands for tailor-made insurance products for constituted groups, or to recruit (local communities or communities recruited on social networks, for example). Start-ups have invested in this niche, which requires a good combination of leading-edge expertise in actuarial science and data science. These new forms of mutualization seem to adequately respond to clients' needs to be recognized in their specificity, as well as to another societal movement for a collective search of solutions and collective intelligence. The approach is virtuous and emphasizes the accountability that will result from belonging to an identified group and will contribute in some kind of prevention. Even if the contribution base should logically be reduced (raising the thresholds of franchises and negotiating capacity for price reductions), insurers could find an advantage in the development of this new distribution method and technical mutualization. A strategy could involve promoting this development by being proactive with communities or creating them via the Web and social networks according to criteria that could facilitate the technical homogeneity of constituted groups. Is it necessary to accompany the peer-to-peer movement at the risk of accelerating the loss of insurable assets, or is it necessary to counter this tendency, which may be temporary?

This active approach would counteract the loss of confidence of some with regard to trusted third parties and prevent them from building solutions to dispense with insurers, for example, the projects of certain communities that use blockchain technology, combined with artificial intelligence and collective intelligence, to replace certain insurance contracts (Dynamis PP and Teambrella in the USA), and this is out of any guarantee and supervision of prudential solvency. Insurers are very attentive to the creativity that surrounds blockchain technology, as it provides many opportunities to test innovative ideas that could be taken up within the framework of an insurance company.

Digital transformation can be envisaged in several ways: by an in-depth reorganization of the company, with the training and maintenance of substantial staff, or by extensive robotization leading to downsizing. The extraordinarily rapid progress of artificial intelligence in voice and text analyses as well as in image analysis will soon make it possible to generalize conversational bots capable of understanding context and thus responding appropriately to questions. Similarly, real-time translation software tools are becoming more efficient. Text classification and summaries as well as software for extracting key information in texts convert some of the work of legal and management services.

Some insurers can back away in view of difficulties they need to overcome in order to internally carry out a real digital transformation. The burden of managing their portfolios, the accumulation of outdated historical strata, habits of organizations and staff who are sometimes poorly responsive to the digital world, all stand as impediments. Why not create a new digital company in parallel with existing companies? Moreover, the regulations encourage new entrants: privacy by design, the ability to instantly provide clients with all the data the company has on them, the ease to meet portability requirements–everything that is so complicated for a historical insurer becomes simple, it is the by design of a new company created intentionally for this.

Another evolution scenario, "as-a-service prevention" model, is based on the idea that technology will significantly reduce risks, which are the rationale behind insurers: autonomous cars, connected homes, etc., would drastically reduce the number of claims and the need for insurance. In fact, even in this scenario, there will be a strong need for cyber risk coverage, which will replace the risks which are disappearing. However, the idea of strategy in this hypothesis would be that the insurer becomes a "prevention specialist", striving to lower the cost of risk and thus the insurance premium, by selling prevention services. The economic model would be completely modified, with the insurer becoming a service company, with an increasingly low share of "promise". One challenge would be charging the service, because consumers are not used to it and have been very unfamiliar with platforms that provide apparently "free" services, whereas in reality, they handsomely pay themselves with the collected data; real digital currency.

4.7.3. *Unavoidable developments*

Regardless of the strategic choice of the insurer, several indispensable actions must be carried out in governance, HR and management: the training of employees, new managerial methods, a change of culture to create an open data of data, a charter on data usage, training on good practices and rules to observe for data security.

Structural reorganizations are essential not only for many insurers to streamline information flows between clusters and break down silos, but also for a more cooperative and cross-functional management, adapted to the new agility needs of companies and operating mode of new generations. Within the new context where strategic risk is increasing and time is accelerating, we must learn to navigate in uncertainty, innovate at the Fintech speed, accept we might make mistakes and change direction very quickly. We need to work on innovation with test and learn practices: failure must no longer be taboo, but be quickly noticed, analyzed and recognized as a building component for the future. Digital transformation has an important social aspect. Some trades will change or even disappear. Employees must be trained to switch to new positions or even train themselves in other occupations and improve their employability. One of the essential points for the security of the insurer's information assets and their image is to involve all staff in the fight against cyber risk. This is not the subject of isolated specialists at the DIS or a DPO or CDO. It is the subject of every corporate "citizen". Not only does it help in reducing insurers' vulnerability to hackers and reduce cyber risk, but it is also the way to make everyone aware of the importance of the heritage of data for the company, of which each is custodian. This is an essential step to understand that everyone must become an actor of their valuation.

4.8. Bibliography

[ACP 16] ACPR, "Autorité de contrôle prudentiel et de résolution". Available at: https://acpr.banque-france.fr/lacpr.html, consulted 16 December 2016.

[CNI 17] CNIL, "Commission nationale de l'informatique et des libertés". Available at: www.cnil.fr, consulted 12 February 2017.

[CNN 17] CNNUM, "Conseil national du numérique". Available at: www.cnnumerique.fr, consulted 26 February 2017.

[COU 16] COUROT P., FOLLY K.A., *Big Data : opportunité ou menace pour l'assurance*, RB Editions, Paris, 2016.

[DUP 15] DUPUIS M., BERTHELÉ E., *Big Data dans l'assurance*, Argus Editions, Paris, 2015.

[FFP 16] FFA, "Chiffres clés". Available at: http://www.ffa-assurance.fr/chiffre-cle, consulted 28 November 2016.

[INS 16] INSTITUT DES ACTUAIRES. Available at: www.institutdesactuaires.com, consulted 25 September 2016.

[OBS 17] OBSERVATOIRE DE L'ÉVOLUTION DES MÉTIERS DE L'ASSURANCE. Available at: www.metiers-assurance.org, consulted 6 January 2017.

[SFD 17] SFDS, "Société française de statistique". Available at: www.sfds.asso.fr, consulted 1 March 2017.

5

Using Big Data in Insurance

5.1. Insurance, an industry particularly suited to the development of big data

5.1.1. *An industry that has developed through the use of data*

5.1.1.1. *Long-standing computerized industry*

The last 60 years have been the occasion for a rapid and comprehensive development of information technology and its uses in all sectors.

The period 1960–1970 was characterized by the adoption of information technology for back-office management purposes in order to record, process and restore large volumes of information previously processed in paper format. Information technology was applied by a very limited number of users, but it already enabled a considerable reduction in processing times and substantial savings.

The development of machines, programming languages and programs during 1970–1980 allowed the development of customized management applications and adoption by a greater number of users. The use of information technology has therefore gradually extended to all areas of management: accounting and management control, execution of payments and cash

---

Chapter written by Emmanuel BERTHELÉ.

management, operational and financial planning, payroll management and more generally human resource-related issues, monitoring and measure of business activity. This democratization of information technology use within companies has gradually led to the development of internal IT services and the diversification of profiles within these services. It should be noted that feedback and some constraints (notably regulatory) are specific to the French market.

The period 1980–1990 was characterized by the diversification of programming languages, progressive miniaturization and standardization of equipment, the development of interoperability between systems and gradual implementation of master plans within companies in order to rationalize investments and adopt a strategic vision for the development of IT resources. At the same time, the number of users within companies continued to increase, and IT was used for almost all current operations, regardless of the size of the company concerned, though at this stage it was not sufficiently developed as regards individuals to constitute a distribution channel.

During 1990–2000, the further development of solutions dedicated to the various information technology uses and the improvement of ergonomics were accompanied by a drop in the cost of equipment. These developments gradually encouraged individuals to equip themselves. For companies, the development of solutions dedicated to storage and data processing contributed to the implementation of data warehouses and the development of data mining methods.

The rapid development of the Internet, despite the explosion of the Internet bubble in 2000, from the second half of the decade greatly contributed to the efforts toward expanding information technology to commercial relationships between companies and also between companies and individuals. Moreover, the emergence of web applications in the period 2000–2010 and the spread of data led to more fragmented modes of urbanization of information systems. In response, the development of methodologies and capacities regarding distributed computing led to increasing flow requirements and the development of a solution-oriented ecosystem.

Since 2010, the development of Internet use through smartphones and the development of social networks have also contributed to the increase in the need for available resources and the diversity of uses of information technology and related services. In addition to data directly generated by users, government incentives for open data contributed to the multiplication and diversification of available data and to the development of stakeholders through their valuation.

The insurance industry was one of the first to make extensive use of information technology, an ideal tool for carrying out numerous, successive and segmented tasks. This adoption has profoundly altered the relationship between insurance companies and their clients, and optimization of management has gradually given way to a real commercial struggle, gradually making insurance a consumer product, in which the positioning of stakeholders has become paramount because of an increasingly competitive environment.

The coming years are moving towards the explosion of the Internet of Things (IoT) and artificial intelligence. The most advanced insurers are already investing heavily on these technologies; therefore, there is no doubt that some of them will gain competitive advantages by improving the quality of their client relationships, increasing their margins and offering their prospects and client guarantees and services that are always more suited to their needs.

The development of Internet accessibility in some developing countries will also help to increase the volume of data generated annually and exploitable in different areas. As their present IT systems are virtually non-existent, they will be able to adopt state-of-the-art technologies directly, especially because the costs associated with these technologies have considerably dropped and, in view of their legal and demographic environments, they witness rapidly developing companies springing up.

5.1.1.2. *An industry whose data is raw material*

From the advent of information technology within the industry, data represent a fundamental asset for insurance companies, the latter being necessary for product pricing, reserving and claims management.

Data are at the heart of the relationship between policyholders and insurers and help in establishing the conditions for their mutual commitment. Insurers conduct their business and manage the risks to which they are subject by anticipating in particular the probability of occurrence of future claims. Knowledge of risk and client behavior is *de facto* a key component in ensuring the sustainability of insurance business, as well as the competitive positioning of insurers and, by extension, the maintenance and development of their market shares.

As regards prevention and claims management, access to an increasing volume of information and the ability to process these data in real time or near real time contribute to a better support of the policyholder and a reduction in claims cost.

Machine learning algorithms, by their ability to process large volumes of data in a data-driven approach and, after industrialization, in an automated manner, logically constitute essential tools in terms of data valuation. They allow the optimal use of data made available through open data and, beyond the data previously collected by insurers, data gathered by the latter through the increasing digitalization of their processes.

5.1.1.3. *An industry whose regulatory framework is an incentive in the area*

Article 82 of Directive 2009/138/EC (Solvency II) introduces data quality requirements for the calculation of technical provisions. Under this Article, insurance and reinsurance companies are required to implement internal processes and procedures to ensure the appropriateness, completeness and accuracy of the data used within this framework.

Articles 19 to 21 of Chapter III, Section 2 of the Delegated Regulation specify these requirements.

The data quality requirements relating to Solvency II potentially constitute a strong limitation on the use of big data for the purpose of calculating technical provisions, particularly in view of the strict requirements with respect to audit trail and complementary requirements dedicated to the use of external data also set out in Article 19 of the Delegated Regulation referred to above. This limitation is one of the factors inducing the use of big data at this limited stage for actuarial purposes.

Criteria	Expected as regards data used in the calculation of technical provisions (TPs)
Completeness	The data include sufficient historical information to assess the characteristics of the underlying risks and identify trends in these risks. They are available for each of the relevant homogeneous risk groups.
Accuracy	The data are free of material errors. They are consistent over time if used for the same estimate. They are recorded in a regular and coherent manner.
Appropriateness	The data are consistent with the use made of them. Their volume and nature are such as to ensure that the estimates made on their basis for the calculation of technical provisions are free of any significant estimation error (that is likely to influence the decision-making or judgment of users of the calculation result, including the supervisory authorities). They are consistent with the assumptions underlying the actuarial and statistical techniques applied to them in the calculation of technical provisions. They adequately reflect the risks to which the insurance or reinsurance company is exposed with regard to its insurance or reinsurance commitments. They are collected, processed and applied in a transparent and structured manner on the basis of a documented procedure. Insurance or reinsurance companies ensure that their data are used consistently over time for the calculation of technical provisions.

Table 5.1. *Solvency II requirements regarding data quality used for the purpose of calculating technical provisions*

The establishment of uniform standards at the European level (Solvency II constitutes only one part of this tendency towards normative standardization, which concerns the entire financial system) and insurance coverage needs of certain segments of the European population should tend towards a standardization of products and the emergence of pan-European products. The behavioral analysis allowed by data science makes it possible for us, within this context, to objectify the formation of new homogeneous risk groups through a data-driven approach.

A first initiative can be put forward regarding the development of pan-European products: at the end of September 2016, Axa Art launched the commercialization of Tailormade, a home insurance product covering real estate, works of art, legal protection, cyber risks and assistance, targeting high-end clients. Upon launching, the product was offered in four European countries (France, Germany, Belgium and the United Kingdom). Four new countries will be introduced in early 2017 (Spain, Italy, Switzerland and the Netherlands).

5.1.2. *Link between data and insurable assets*

5.1.2.1. *Insurability*

Risk, which is the raw material of insurance, is the confrontation of hazards with human, material and, by extension, financial stakes.

DEFINITION.– *To be insurable, a risk must be random, futural, lawful, independent of the will of the policyholder and sufficiently common to be subject to calculation of its probability of occurrence without being almost certain.*

The digitalization of the relationship between insurers and policyholders significantly increases the frequency of data collection, the matching capacities of data collected with external data increase the diversity of the available information and the machine learning methods make it possible to identify the most discriminatory variables in order to predict a behavior or the occurrence of a given risk. In effect, the vision of risks tends to be refined and price variations may occur:

– infra-annual variations related to changes in the consumption habits of policyholders during the year (for example, seasonality of automobile use or occupation of a secondary residence). Externally, pricing and, by extension, insurance to the act, based on data from connected objects, could be envisaged;

– refined segmentation of guarantees within a contract and ability of the policyholder to underwrite only a part of the guarantees offered (for example, home insurance contracts often include lump-sum guarantees that may be unsuitable for young clients).

Beyond the modulation of existing products and guarantees, the development of guarantees for risks hitherto considered as uninsurable could be envisaged due to the availability of new data sources. Finally, the insurance of emerging risks (for example, cyber risk) is also facilitated.

5.1.2.2. *Concept of pooling*

Pooling is a key insurance principle. It involves apportioning the cost of claims arising from the occurrence of a hazard between the members of a group potentially subject to it and having, in fact, taken out insurance to protect themselves.

Insurance organizes with fairness financial solidarity between persons constituting a homogeneous risk group with regard to the hazard considered: mutuality. Prices adjust according to the evolution of risk, and mutuality is penalized in case of fraud from its members.

A better knowledge of risk relating to the different insured homogeneous risks groups allows the refinement of the price of proposed guarantees by making it correspond exactly to the risk to which the insurer is subject because of the commitments undertaken.

5.1.2.3. *The fantasy of personalized prices*

The advent of big data in insurance has given rise to a belief in the ability of insurers to have a very precise knowledge of risk such that the price of guarantees could be personalized.

Although the idea of price personalization may seem attractive at first sight, several points, however, run counter to it.

First, personalization implies full and complete knowledge of the risk factors constituting the hazard. However, the acquisition of such a level of knowledge is impossible (influence of the environment, instability in behavior of policyholders, etc.), and a pooling, possibly finer, but minimal within a homogeneous risk group, will always be technically necessary to ensure the viability of products and proposed guarantees.

Moreover, since this personalization eliminates pooling between policyholders making up a homogeneous risk group, only temporal pooling, policyholder by policyholder, of the risk incurred would remain, and would have two main consequences:

– some policyholders may be inclined to privately organize their own temporal pooling of assets without resorting to insurance but by prioritizing financial products;

– others, for whom the price would have become prohibitive, would be inclined not to underwrite an insurance which, beyond the potentially dramatic consequences for them in the event of claims, poses a real societal problem because of the resulting inability of policyholders to pay potential damages inflicted on third parties.

Finally, as demonstrated in an article by Charpentier *et al.* [CHA 15] over-segmentation (and by extension, price personalization), although leading to an increase in the per capita profitability of policyholders maintained in portfolio, results in a competitive market for the creation of a niche market, and the insured population being reduced to a given insurer (policyholders most penalized by the price changes opting for an insurer with a less fine segmentation) leads to a decrease in its turnover and overall profitability in the entire insured portfolio.

5.1.2.4. *Adaptation of insurance to uses thanks to the available data*

Changes in lifestyle and consumption significantly contribute to the increase in the volume of available data. The digitalization of activities is only permitted by the adoption by policyholders of a way of life where all services must be permanently available, regardless of the location and in multichannel.

This transition to an economy of immediacy is accompanied by the development of collaboration and continuous assessment of goods consumed. Insurance is no exception to the trend and is increasingly becoming a consumer good for which the valuations provided by insured clients will allow a greater adaptation of the guarantees and services offered.

Similar to the trend observed in other sectors, insured clients tend to increasingly seek tailor-made services and guarantees that are perfectly adapted to their needs. In this context, they seem more and more inclined to make their data available if this can allow a greater personification of the proposals made by insurance companies.

The growth in the volume of product data is exponential, each year the volume of data produced is more than twice the volume produced the previous year such that 90% of the existing data were generated over the past 2 years.

5.1.3. *Multiplication of data sources of potential interest*

5.1.3.1. *Data directly available to the insurer*

Current developments do not call into question the acquisition of certain data traditionally collected by insurers:

– data relating to policyholders, although pricing restrictions may exist in this area (for example, after the gender directive, in car insurance, gender can no longer be discriminatory as regards pricing, although it may continue to be as such with regard to reserving);

– data related to insured persons or property;

– data related to contracts and guarantees subscribed;

– data related to premiums paid and previous claims incurred by the policyholder and more generally to the different financial flows existing between the insurer and the insured.

The digitalization of activities, however, creates two antagonistic tendencies:

– the simplification of the underwriting processes tends to limit the data requested from policyholders when underwriting. However, the ability to match external data will compensate for the loss of information generated;

– the multiplication of contact channels (particularly, websites and mobile applications) and the adaptation of insurance offerings to the economy of use multiply opportunities for contacts between insured persons and insurers and contribute to the increase of exploitable data by insurers, both in terms of frequency of data acquisition and diversity (connection logs on the insurer's website in particular or telephone exchanges that can be valued via the use of speech to text and semantic analysis).

These two trends do not offset each other. The volume of data available to policyholders and their exposure to insured risks are significantly increasing such that insurers implement technological and financial means to make use of them.

5.1.3.2. *Connected objects data*

Although the data derived from connected objects is considered an important source of information as regards the behavior of the insured, and because they allow a very detailed analysis over time of how they use the connected object, their use for insurance purposes still remains marginal.

Data related to the quantified self cannot at this stage be considered as usable for insurance purposes because of existing regulatory restrictions and a limited desire by the insured to make them available to insurers. Data related to connected cars, although already being collected, are still underexploited.

However, the strong development of these objects and their generalization to all types of objects planned by 2020 should make them sufficiently incorporated into ways of life and consumption habits so that regulatory changes and a more natural way of making the data available are envisaged.

The issue for insurers to settle will rather concern the direction of their investments in this area, since not all the developed objects will witness the same level of success, the connection tendency of certain objects may sometimes lead to something ridiculous and the insured could adopt these objects to make primary use of the objects themselves and not for their secondary use for insurance purposes.

5.1.3.3. *Social network data*

Given their massive adoption by the population and the considerable volume of information they carry, personal and professional social networks, at first impression, appeared to be an important source of data to insurers, and at the time of awareness of the potential contribution of big data to the market, some insurers envisaged to value them.

At present, the enthusiasm for this potential repository of data has, to a large extent, abated. Although the available data are indeed numerous and potentially varied, they are, beyond the problems related to the use of personal data, also largely biased, many of them reflecting what the user wishes to communicate to its network. They are, in fact, more representative of appearance than reality and difficult to use for the purpose of studying behavior or analyzing risk.

5.1.3.4. *External data made available*

Beyond the data directly available through the relationships between insurers and their insured and data from connected objects, external data sources can be of substantial interest to both banking and insurance stakeholders.

In this context, the data made available by certain public bodies such as the INSEE or certain climatology/meteorological websites in particular may be of great interest for the understanding of the typology of the insured or exposure to the risks of insured property.

The data made available, subject to the payment, by some private organizations such as Bloomberg or certain aggregators could also be valued, in particular for the purpose of understanding the macroeconomic environment and behavioral changes it engenders over time as regards policyholders.

Given the existing incentives for making data available (French Lemaire Law, for example), financial sector stakeholders are logically led to consider their use and the implementation of a monitoring system dedicated to the supervision over time of data made available.

NOTE.– Even if the volume of data available and the capacities induced in price refinement increase considerably, price personalization is neither fully feasible nor desirable for insurers, insured persons and society in general.

5.2. Examples of application in different insurance activities

This section aims to highlight existing examples, examples under development or potential examples of the application of big data relevant in insurance within the meaning of the interest of the service and guarantees for the insured, gain in competitiveness or for risk management for insurers.

These examples, while varied, are in no way an exhaustive list of possible applications of big data in insurance, and it is up to each insurer to analyze the potential contribution:

– of its own data, as regards both already used data and data not yet valued or data which may be collected but is yet to be;

– of external data accessible through open data, the purchase of data from external partners or implementation of sensors within the framework of a connected insurance offer.

The matching of the various data, beyond the intrinsic interest specific to each of them, makes it possible to generate new data that may be of significant interest through feature engineering and to implement a real data-driven approach limiting the cognitive biases on the explanatory character of the different variables in the explanation of a given behavior.

Moreover, given the current context conducive to the emergence and increasingly rapid adoption of technological innovations, it goes without saying that these contributions are still limited at this stage and will be amplified by the cross-matching of big data with other emerging innovations, including:

– blockchain and smart contracts;

– artificial intelligence and the emergence of bots and chatbots.

Other innovations will contribute to the exponential generation of new data sources, including:

– the development of connected objects;

– the emergence of platforms for the collection of personal data.

Finally, if the data generated so far are mainly due to mature markets, the contribution of emerging countries is set to explode from 2017.

5.2.1. *Use for pricing purposes and product offer orientation*

Through the matching of external data with relative data, products and guarantees, policyholders and their claims, it is possible, using machine learning algorithms, to identify the most discriminatory variables for pricing purposes in a data-driven manner.

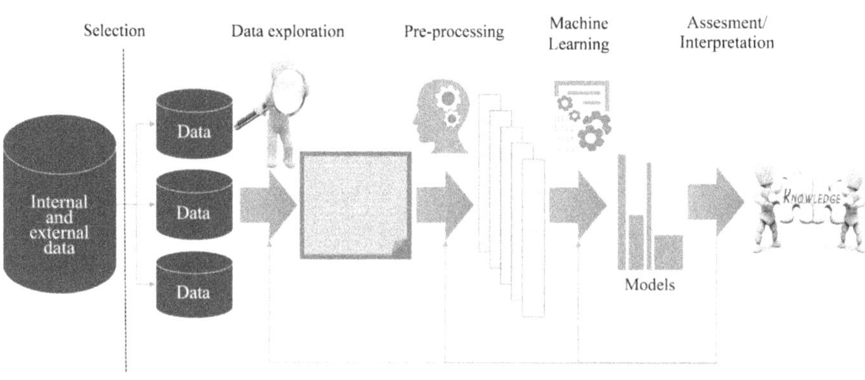

Figure 5.1. *Classical data science process (source: DataSquare)*

The studies carried out may have different purposes:

– offering products and guarantees adapted to client targets on which an insurer wishes to develop;

– challenging the previously used price variables, the latter most often established on the basis of the only available data in the portfolio;

– simplifying the underwriting process: increasingly, the simplicity of underwriting insurance contracts is a factor promoting the transformation of online estimates into duly underwritten insurance contracts (Lemonade, for example, greatly complements the data requested within the framework of its underwriting process with matched external data);

– establishing a refined price in terms of price zoning (micro-zoning, review of existing zones), where the price applied depends on the location of the insured, as can be the case for car or home insurance.

In terms of pricing, process optimization and orientation of insurers product offers, possibilities are numerous and experiments and projects multiply under constraints, however, of meeting compliance requirements with regard to the use of personal data and data matching. The cross-matching of insurance and banking data by bank insurers, for example, although it may be carried out for research and experimentation purposes, requires the implementation of a data exchange protocol that is legally binding at the group level.

Orientation of offerings is one of the areas in which the reciprocal expertise of actuaries and data scientists will be the most complementary and source of both mutual enrichment and value-adding for insurance companies. Insurance fundamentals such as pricing and reserving, due to the technical and regulatory requirements they raise, will logically remain, for the time being, the sole preserve of actuaries.

5.2.2. *Automobile insurance and telematics*

Telematic data collected through sensors connected to the diagnostic socket of insured vehicles (a more reliable and more informative means of collecting data than collection via mobile phones, within a given timeframe) allow a spatio-temporal analysis of the risk borne by policyholders, in view of their driving behavior and the environment in which they operate (weather, traffic, road conditions, etc.).

At this stage, the data collected make it possible to establish driving scores which allow policyholders to change their behavior while driving and they also take the gamification of driving more into consideration than preventive action. This information is also used to provide the insured with a discount on their car insurance premium in contracts that are progressively evolving to better match the risk incurred. The latest major changes as regards pay as you drive and pay how you drive are presented in Table 5.2.

Pay X you drive		
X	**Description of the guarantee**	**Initiators**
X = As	Annual modulation of the insurance price according to the mileage	Amaguiz (2008) Axa and Allianz (2009)
X = How	Monthly modulation of the insurance price according to the driver's driving behavior Currently, driving scoring and premium modulation "determined by an expert"	Axa and Allianz (2015)

Table 5.2. *Existing pay "X" you drive guarantees*

From the data collected so far, it is difficult to objectively provide reductions granted according to the claims observed, since France lags behind the development of these types of products compared to other European countries such as Germany or Italy. Also, the reductions granted are attributed on the basis of expert judgments, both concerning the percentages of reduction and the identification of driving behaviors likely to limit the risk of accident.

Moreover, in addition to the study of driving behavior, the data collected must make it possible, through matching with external geospatial data, to obtain a better knowledge of the environment in which the insured operates, which beyond simple price modulation allows the development of new services and preventive actions, for example:

– informing policyholders in case of risk of hail and incentive to return their car;

– encouraging policyholders to take a break after excessively long driving periods;

– calling of emergency services in the event of an accident or real-time assistance in case of a breakdown;

– informing policyholders of the risks associated with their itinerary.

If initially insured persons were reluctant to share their data with their insurer, it seems that the acceptance to share such data would be facilitated by the development of such services and preventive actions. Furthermore, the latter will constitute a lever of growth and retention ability for the insurers proposing them and will contribute to an improvement of their image. Indeed, where automobile insurers mainly intervened in the past in the event of a claim, or under tragic circumstances, they were able to intervene upstream of their realization by allowing their policyholders to protect themselves without witnessing inconvenience.

Beyond this desire to improve their image among their policyholders, insurers may also contribute to the improvement of road safety policies by indicating, for example, the most accidental locations.

5.2.3. *Index-based insurance of weather-sensitive events*

Index-based insurance allows the protection of income related to weather-sensitive activities. This type of insurance is logically destined to develop because of the following:

– evolution of the hazard linked to climate change;

– evolution of stakes: increase in insured amounts.

This type of insurance has a notable feature insofar as compensation is triggered when a generally meteorological index exceeds a previously established threshold. Insurance thus covers a return more than it covers actual damages suffered.

It may not be enforced against index-based insurance as the policy is not really in the nature of an insurance in the sense that it does not necessarily compensate for a loss. In reality, index-based insurance checks the insurability criteria for a risk (defined in section 5.1.2.1), the insured risk being in this case the attaining of the criterion defined as trigger of the insurance benefit, such as living benefit guarantees in life insurance.

The indexes make it possible to materialize the jeopardy of return and to define the level of compensation. The latter is automatically triggered on their basis through a simplified declaration and settlement process. In this sense, the functioning is comparable to smart contracts, which are called upon to develop through blockchains.

Given the functioning of these guarantees, it is noted, however, that if compensation without damage is possible, an incorrect calibration of the index trigger level may result in non-compensation for actual damage suffered. In this sense, data science can prove to be a valuable tool for defining the thresholds for triggering the guarantees proposed on the basis of a history of claims and satellite data or derived from weather stations.

Some operators, such as Meteo Protect, develop these types of insurance solutions and progressively extend their range to various weather-sensitive activities (energy, transport, tourism, etc.). For example, the agricultural industry has been able to benefit from guarantees suited to the operating losses potentially generated as a result of weather variations.

More traditional stakeholders in the insurance industry (Swiss Re, Allianz, Axa Corporate Solutions, Pacifica, etc.) have also positioned themselves in recent years to offer these types of guarantees. Given the expertise still required at this stage, the proposed guarantees concern a diversity of risks and limited geographical coverage, but the possible automation of calibration of this type of guarantees through the use of data science should contribute to their development.

Beyond the weather-sensitive economic activities, growing urbanization as well as population growth and densification, human and financial stakes associated with climate and weather tend to increase. A better understanding of their impacts helps to improve risk management in terms of insurance as well as the development of suitable risk prevention and mitigation policies at the level of public authorities.

5.2.4. *Orientation of savings in life insurance in a context of low interest rates*

In the current low interest rate context, insurers offering savings products such as life insurance are naturally interested in achieving an in-depth understanding of the behavioral dynamics of unit-linked investment of their policyholders.

Data science, through the valorization of both internal and external data, and the use of machine learning algorithms can make it possible to obtain such an understanding. However, depending on the accessibility of data, the level of progress of stakeholders and the product and portfolio characteristics, approaches to be implemented, results achieved and the uses that can be made of them differ.

The added-value brought about by the matching of external data, notably relating to the economic environment, varies according to the cyclical nature of the various predicted acts. Thus, although the contribution is limited for the prediction of total surrenders, it is, however, increasing according to whether partial surrenders, premiums or switches are involved.

The pitch of the prediction model is also significant. Indeed, if few insurers have been able to record the realization of cyclical trade-offs through classical modeling carried out with an annual pitch, a monthly prediction made using data science and matching external economic data helps to better capture such behavior. While the interest may be considered limited, although existing, with a view to feeding a prospective model, it is different for marketing interest, such a prediction enabling the identification of efficient incentives and taking them into account in commercial policy.

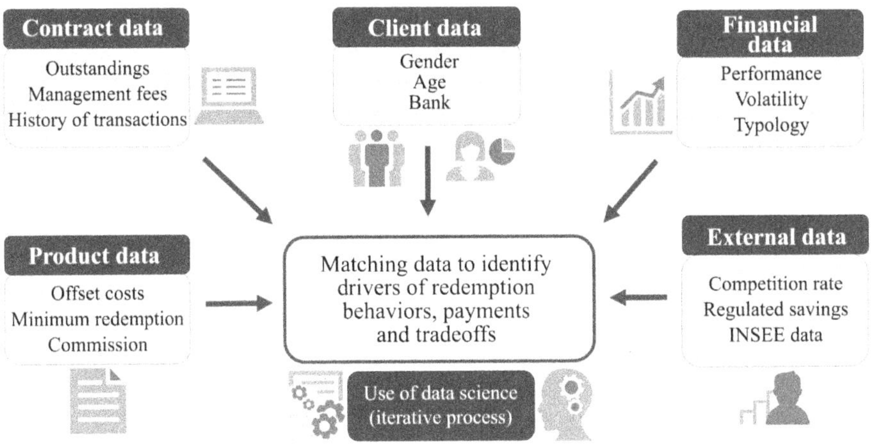

Figure 5.2. *Type of matched data for the study of behaviors in life insurance (source: DataSquare)*

Beyond a precise use that allows an understanding of the historical behavior of policyholders, it is appropriate that it should be possible to easily reuse the implemented algorithms. For example, the past decade has witnessed an almost continuous drop in interest rates and an unprecedented financial crisis. In effect, the future cyclical behavior of policyholders may potentially differ from the past behaviors apprehended on history via a recourse to supervised learning. The regular reuse of algorithms makes it possible to capture behavioral changes, evolutions which will not fail to occur with the rise in interest rates expected due to the actions of the Federal Reserve in the United States and the progressive stoppage of quantitative easing scheduled for 2017 at the level of the ECB.

Similarly, data science allows the analysis and prediction of banking behaviors regarding deposits, partial or total prepayments or renegotiations. The studies carried out can allow a better feeding of bank ALM models and, through the use of appropriate metrics, a more efficient orientation of the commercial policy through better client targeting.

5.2.5. *Fight against fraud*

As regards insurance, there are almost as many types of fraud as there are types of commitments. However, two instances are logically more sensitive: underwriting and submissions of claims.

Underwriting may be an opportunity for a declaration overestimating the insured property, in particular with regard to multi-risk home insurance. Submissions of claims may be an opportunity for overestimating the claim incurred or even of the declaration of a claim not actually incurred.

Fraud can be individual or networked and, where appropriate, the identification of the network as a whole, which can be realized through interaction graphs between stakeholders, contributes greatly to the effectiveness of the anti-fraud mechanism.

The stakes in the fight against fraud are numerous:

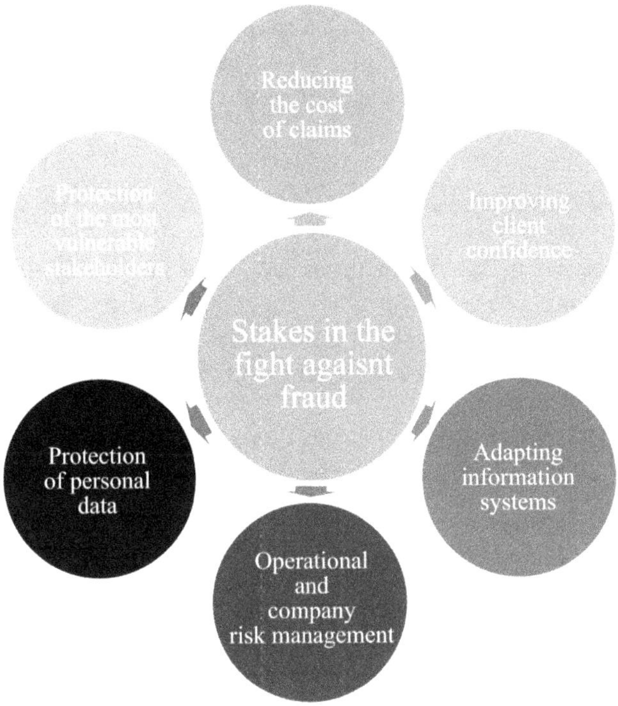

Figure 5.3. *Stakes in the fight against fraud (source: Optimind Winter [OPT 16])*

As regards anti-fraud measures, even if the ability to process data in real time or near real time is paramount, it must be pointed out that algorithms cannot be the only tools used to identify fraudsters: they allow the identification of profiles of potential fraudsters for which investigations must be carried out.

Two main approaches can be explored to take advantage of data science in the fight against fraud:

– a classical approach involving the implementation of a traditional fraud detection process (where fraudsters' profiles are based on intuitive drivers), identification of cases of proven fraud, use of supervised learning to refine the identification of profiles of fraudsters/non-fraudsters and reiteration;

– the initialization of the traditional approach process can be replaced by an alternative approach to identify the profiles for which the submitted claims vary significantly from the theoretical claims. The identification of profiles may be done within this framework through a data-driven approach. The rest of the process is comparable to the traditional approach.

5.2.6. *Asset management*

Machine learning algorithms are already used in different high-frequency trading algorithms. At this stage, however, their use for asset management purposes for insurance is very marginal, as the investment objectives of insurance do not respond to the same temporality.

Despite this observation, various uses that may contribute to the management of investments can be envisaged:

– regarding strategic allocation (for example, managing an intersectoral allocation of corporate investments);

– regarding tactical allocation (for example, managing an intrasectoral allocation of corporate assets by anticipating credit rating migrations).

These examples are not exhaustive, and the wealth and diversity of the available financial information and the ability to link the consideration of ALM constraints with the latter should enhance the development of the use of data science for investment management purposes.

5.2.7. *Reinsurance*

Traditionally, insurers wishing to market new guarantees can rely on the support of reinsurance stakeholders. The latter, with data from different insurers and significant resources, can develop a refined vision of risk compared to what would be that of non-supported insurers wishing to enter a new market or under the cover of emerging risks (cyber risk, for example).

There should be renewed interest in this relatively widespread approach regarding development of new guarantees given the new ability of reinsurers to match the data of different insurers with each other and to match all of these data with external data, which help to refine the understanding of the influence of risk factors in the triggering of claims.

Thus, reinsurers should assert their position as support to insurers in the development and commercialization of new types of guarantees and products.

NOTE.– Data science allows the optimization of available data to be used for a wide variety of purposes, particularly in the identification of risk factors and the understanding of behaviors. Given the large number of potential use cases, their identification and prioritization must be in the hands of the trades (marketing/distribution, actuarial product, risk management, etc.) so as to maximize the added-value for the insurance company.

5.3. New professions and evolution of induced organizations for insurance companies

5.3.1. *New professions related to data management, processing and valuation*

Developing the valuation of data and data science tends to generate new needs for insurers and new professions:

Although several companies have in recent years implemented a chief digital officer function to support the digitalization of their activities, the latter logically will eventually disappear once the digital culture has been sufficiently implanted within the different business departments.

The success of the chief digital officer results in the disappearance of this function.

Functions	Prerogatives
Chief data officer	– coordination of data collection (identification of data relevant to the company, financing of action plans, purchase of software packages or data, etc.); – organization of data sharing with the different departments, in particular the business departments; – production of business-oriented recommendations; – ensuring the observance of ethics as regards data use.
Data scientist	– contribution to the assessment of business needs; – identification, cleaning and preparation of internal and external data, structured or unstructured; – implementation of algorithms or assemblies of machine learning algorithms; – formulation of hypotheses to be tested via the developed algorithms; – supporting the industrialization of experiments carried out.
Big data architect	– construction of distributed computer architectures, data integration, easing of data accessibility and optimization of performance; – adaptation of IT architecture to processing needs (real time, for example).
Data visualization expert	– using data visualization tools to implement renditions (dashboards, mappings, synthetic indicators, etc.) allowing the understanding of information and decision-making.
Data analyst	– organization, summarizing and translation of massive information.
Master data manager	– acquisition and optimization of the information available within the company in order to enhance its optimal use (data related to products, guarantees and services offered, client and contract data, regulations, etc.); – ensuring the legitimate use of data and their proper integration into information systems.
Data protection officer	– ensuring the protection of personal data and supporting those responsible for processing (cross-cutting function requiring computer, law and communication skills).

Table 5.3. *Main data professions (the list is not necessarily exhaustive but the name may vary according to organizations)*

5.3.2. *Development of partnerships between insurers and third-party companies*

Recent progress in technological development is such that insurance companies may not be able to invest on all the technologies developed. Insurance companies committed to their objective of securing the stakes associated with the risks related to the lives of policyholders support the development of consumption habits, in particular the development of collaborative economy.

Thus, some insurers have established partnerships with different stakeholders (for example, almost all car-pooling websites have a privileged partnership with an insurer), set up seed capital or take part in round-table meetings organized by innovative companies.

Beyond the laboratories and the many experiments they implement directly, these partnerships are an important lever to take advantage of the evolutions in progress while limiting and diversifying the risk associated with their investments.

5.4. Development constraints

5.4.1. *Constraints specific to the insurance industry*

5.4.1.1. *Constraints related to the regulation of the insurance industry*

The implementation of Solvency II, although having brought substantial progress and market standardization in terms of risk management, constitutes an impediment to the adoption of big data because of the constraints they impose regarding the use of data.

Pillars 1 and 3 induce strong constraints on audit trails and data used for behavioral modeling purposes.

Within the framework of the ORSA, on the other hand, greater use of big data could be envisaged such as to accurately represent the risk profile of insurance or reinsurance companies by resorting to behavior laws established through machine learning algorithms that are more effective though less auditable than traditional GLMs. In this context, the differential of laws used would have to be taken into account in the ORSA third assessment: deviation of the risk profile.

5.4.1.2. *Constraints related to the French CNIL*

On November 12 2014, the Commission Nationale de l'Informatique et des Libertés (*National Commission on Information Technologies and Freedom*) (CNIL) and all the professional federations concerned presented the compliance package for the insurance industry. A dedicated "compliance club" has also been created to ensure that it remains operational over time.

The compliance package is a tool for regularizing the use of personal data, which covers:

– a working method allowing the collaboration of insurance and public actors as well as potentially related users and the CNIL such as to bring out good practices and respond to issues specific to the insurance industry;

– a regulation method for the CNIL aimed at establishing a sectoral reference framework for the processing of personal data around rules and good practices, expressed through legal means (simplified standards, single authorizations, recommendations, etc.) and operational procedures as well as organizational processes.

Overall, it aims at providing legal protection to professionals by giving tangible incentives on how to comply with specific texts and procedures and to simplify formalities as far as current law permits, using exemptions, simplified standards and single authorizations.

The insurance package integrates various practical sheets on specific topics:

Practical sheets	Topic
Sheet 1	Award, management and execution of insurance contracts
Sheet 2	Commercial management of clients and prospects for the insurance industry
Sheet 3	Collection of the registration number in the directory (NIR) and consultation of the national directory of identification of individuals (RNIPP)
Sheet 4	Collection of offense, conviction or security measures data
Sheet 5	Fight against fraud

Table 5.4. *Practical sheets falling within the CNIL insurance package*

The insurance package is based on the requirements of Law No. 78-17 of January 6, 1978 as amended relating to information technology, files and civil liberties (so-called Data Protection Act), but updating will necessarily be done with the evolution of the normative framework.

5.4.1.3. *Constraints related to stakeholder priorities*

Since the investment capacities of a significant portion of insurance industry stakeholders are limited, their priority is not constantly focused on innovation and the development of approaches and methodologies to generate value.

Thus, regulatory compliance work related to Solvency II and product-oriented regulations (French Hamon and Eckert laws, PRIIPS European laws, etc.) and soon investments related to the requirements on IFRS 17 will drain part of the industry's investment.

Moreover, the gradual concentration of the market and coming together of certain stakeholders have generated political and organizational constraints which hardly enhance the development of data science and big data, and at the level of longstanding established groups, the positioning of data initiatives within the organization remains a topical issue. However, these constraints should only be temporal and the groups should obtain a longer-term advantage because of the volumes and diversity of data available to them.

5.4.2. *Constraints non-specific to the insurance industry*

5.4.2.1. *Regulatory constraints*

Beyond the experiments conducted or in progress, stakeholders privilege IT- and compliance-oriented works. At this stage, very few industrialization initiatives can really be brought forward in the insurance industry.

As regards compliance, one of the main constraints is the observance of compliance requirements imposed by the GDPR (General Data Protection Regulation), adopted on April 27, 2016. In France, constraints related to the GDPR constitute an important normative update. The current reference framework for the use of personal data is the Data Protection Act of January 6, 1978.

In addition to specifying new definitions around personal data, the Regulation introduces new obligations and responsibilities for stakeholders.

Terms	Definitions
Sensitive data	Data that directly or indirectly reveal racial or ethnic origins, political, philosophical or religious opinions, trade union membership of persons or relating to health or sex life
Health data	Any information relating to the physical or mental health of a person or to the provision of health services to that person
Medical data	Data that reveal or are likely to reveal the pathological condition of persons, produced or collected during a prevention, diagnosis or care activity

Table 5.5. *New definitions distinguishing the data sensitivity level*

Thus, the data processing officer must ensure the implementation of proactive measures aimed at preventing as early as possible the infringement of human rights.

Requirements	Definitions
Data protection from the design stage	"The data processing officer must implement, both at the time of determining the processing means and at the time of processing itself, appropriate technical and organizational measures, such as pseudonymization, which are intended to implement the principles relating to data protection, for example, the minimization of data in an effective manner and to match the processing of the necessary guarantees to meet the requirements of these Regulations as well as to protect the rights of the data subject".
Data protection by default	The data processing officer shall implement the appropriate technical and organizational measures to ensure that, by default: – only the personal data necessary for each specific processing purpose are processed. This applies to the amount of personal data collected, the extent of their processing, their shelf life and accessibility (data minimization principle); – personal data are not made accessible to an undetermined number of natural persons without the involvement of the natural person concerned (personal data access limitation principle).
Risk analysis and impact study	Prior to any processing likely to present a high risk, carrying out a privacy impact study. This includes processing that present specific risks such as "the processing of information relating to [...] health". Throughout the data's lifecycle, carrying out an objective assessment of risk with respect to the processing nature, scope, context and objectives.

Table 5.6. *Data security requirements (Source: Optimind Winter, GDPR publication of September 2016 [OPT 16])*

Some public and private sector organizations are obliged to appoint a data protection officer (DPO) in charge of enhancing the observance of constraints as regards data protection by the various parties involved, by specifically using a data dictionary and a register of processing activities identifying, for each processing, the internal or external stakeholders, purposes, categories of data and persons concerned including the deletion periods.

Given the new requirements stipulated by the GDPR, all banking and insurance stakeholders must logically, following an impact assessment measuring the compliance deviation, implement a review of their current personal data protection mechanism by the deadline of May 25, 2018, date of immediate implementation of the Regulation. In addition to the appointment of the DPO, various organizational and governance projects are being initiated or are to be quickly considered for all banking and insurance stakeholders.

As a complement to the GDPR, the French Military Planning Act also defines specific constraints for organizations of vital importance. Some banking and insurance stakeholders may therefore be subject to additional requirements to those laid down by the GDPR.

Finally, the Digital Republic Act, which emphasizes a proactive policy with regard to open data at the level of national public services, the right to oblivion and data portability, must still be the subject of implementing decrees. It constitutes both a constraint and a source of opportunity given the new data sources that will be made available and the additional requirements that it entails.

NOTE.– Within the meaning of Law No. 78-17 of January 6, 1978 relating to information technology, files and freedoms (version consolidated on June 2, 2016), personal data means "all information relating to an identified natural person or which may be directly or indirectly identified, by reference to an identification number or to one or more of its own elements".

5.4.2.2. *Cultural constraints*

There may exist different cultural constraints in the adoption of data valuation and the use of machine learning:

– beyond normative constraints, sensitivity to the collection and use of personal data: policyholders seem more inclined to allow insurers to use their data, provided they have price offers or services adapted to them. Significant differences may exist between populations or population segments, so this wealth of data remains logically underexploited;

– development of open data: in France, a proactive policy exists, but this is not necessarily the case in other countries;

– the weak development of test and learn culture and valuation of failure: if in the United States failure is often considered a prerequisite for success, in Europe, this culture is less widespread and insurers often wish to identify, prior to their implementation, uses of machine learning likely to have a substantial contribution.

The implementation of experiments, regularly designated as proof of concept or proof of value, makes it possible to highlight the contribution of data science approaches prior to their industrialization. However, although the algorithms implemented are often designed to be scalable, the ROI (return on investment) obtained is not always scalable.

5.4.3. *Constraints, according to the purposes, with regard to the types of algorithms used*

The auditability requirements relating to certain processes (calculation of technical provisions and pricing in particular) imply that certain algorithms cannot be used to their full potential. It is thus possible to use them for the identification of discriminatory variables, but the final calibration must ultimately be carried out using algorithms allowing greater auditability (generalized linear model, for example).

Thus, random forests or gradient boosting algorithms, while providing convincing prediction results, cannot generally be used for pricing or risk management purposes. More marketing- and distribution-oriented approaches are less constrained and can benefit from them, and beyond insurers' initial desire to optimize their business processes, these constraints partly explain the delay in the adoption of data science in risk management.

The growing adoption and dissemination of data science methodologies may ultimately lead to a relaxation of constraints subject to a documented justification of the strong predictive capacities of these algorithms and highlighting of their utility.

5.4.4. *Scarcity of profiles and main differences with actuaries*

The French need for data scientists is estimated between 2000 and 3000 persons per year, in all sectors. Despite the development of adapted training in recent years, it is clear that this need is, at this stage, far from being covered.

Training courses to acquire skills in data science and insurance are even fewer. In addition, the French Institute of Actuaries has implemented a training program dedicated to the application of data science in insurance, accessible to both actuaries and actuarial researchers.

Other training courses are now available, but there are still very few of them, and the acquisition of business knowledge necessary for data scientists to reveal the full potential of their know-how is most often done directly in companies.

Thus, data scientists, logically, at least have to first work with actuaries to benefit from their knowledge of the processes related to insurance, product specificities and guarantees. However, although the collaboration between figure-lovers is easily established and the skills of the different parties can gradually be brought together regarding certain items, the average profiles of the two professions still remain relatively distinct, as shown in Table 5.7.

Since anything scarce becomes expensive, data scientists with sufficient training are often entitled to the most competitive packages. Also, some stakeholders, although aware of the strategic nature of the valuation of their data and the opportunities that may arise, are still reluctant to align their compensation proposals with market standards and consequently find it difficult to recruit. The maturity of offerings dedicated to insurance in terms of data science and the multiplication of training courses for the data scientist profession should make it possible to gradually compensate for these difficulties.

Actuary	**Data scientist**
MAIN PREROGATIVES	
Pricing Reserving Carrying out of inventories Observance of regulatory and prudential constraints Implementation and use of projection models	Data source monitoring Business intelligence solutions monitoring Implementation and use of predictive algorithms Identification of client behavior Optimization of client value
Contribution to product creation Contribution to risk management Data quality management	

EXPECTED LEVEL OF THE MAIN SKILLS REQUIRED	
Knowledge of internal data	
+++	+++
Sensitivity to the use of external data	
+	+++
Product knowledge	
+++	++
Client knowledge	
++	+++
Accounting skills	
+	–
Technical and financial skills	
+++	+
Business intelligence skills	
+	+++
Predictive algorithm	
+	+++
Prospective modeling and dedicated tools	
+++	+
Legal constraints	
+	+
Strategic management	
++	–
Observance of decision-making/governance processes	
++	++
Note: The weights of the different prerogatives and expected levels are indicative; they may vary from one organization to another (mainly depending on their size and insurance activities practiced).	

Table 5.7. *Skills expected of actuaries and data scientists (source: Optimind Winter, Big Data Book in Insurance, 2014)*

5.5. Bibliography

[ARG 17] ARGUS DE L'ASSURANCE, "Métiers : l'assurance indicielle, une solution prometteuse", available at: http://www.argusdelassurance.com/metiers/metiers-l-assurance-indicielle-une-solution-prometteuse.98859, consulted 2 February, 2017.

[CHA 15] CHARPENTIER A., DENUIT M., ROMUALD ELIE R., "Segmentation et mutualisation: Les deux faces d'une même pièce?", *Risques*, no. 103, pp. 19–23, November 2015.

[CNI 17] CNIL, "Assurance: création d'un club conformité", available at: https://www.cnil.fr/fr/assurance-creation-dun-club-conformite, consulted 2 February, 2017.

[DAT 16] DATASQUARE, Optimind Winter, Retour d'expérience comparé de 2 POCs Data Science sur l'analyse du comportement en Epargne, 100% Data Science, 2016.

[DUP 14] DUPUIS M., BERTHELÉ E., *Le Big Data dans l'Assurance*, L'Argus Editions, Antony, 2014.

[OPT 16] OPTIMIND WINTER, Entrée en vigueur du règlement européen sur la protection des données à caractère personnel, September 2016.

List of Authors

Emmanuel Berthelé
Optimind Winter
Paris
France

Romain Billot
IMT Atlantique
Brest
France

Cécile Bothorel
IMT Atlantique
Brest
France

Marine Corlosquet-Habart
EURIA
Brest
France

Jacques Janssen
Solvay Business School
Brussels
Belgium

Philippe Lenca
IMT Atlantique
Brest
France

Florence Picard
Institut des Actuaires
Paris
France

Jean-Charles Pomerol
UPMC
Paris
France

Gilbert Saporta
CNAM
Paris
France

Franck Vermet
EURIA
Brest
France

Index

P, R, S

T, U

Other titles from

ISTE

in

Innovation, Entrepreneurship and Management

2017

AÏT-EL-HADJ Smaïl
The Ongoing Technological System
(Smart Innovation Set – Volume 11)

BAUDRY Marc, DUMONT Béatrice
Patents: Prompting or Restricting Innovation?
(Smart Innovation Set – Volume 12)

BÉRARD Céline, TEYSSIER Christine
Risk Management: Lever for SME Development and Stakeholder Value Creation

CHALENÇON Ludivine
Location Strategies and Value Creation of International Mergers and Acquisitions

CHAUVEL Danièle, BORZILLO Stefano
The Innovative Company: An Ill-defined Object
(Innovation Between Risk and Reward Set – Volume 1)

CORSI Patrick
Going Past Limits To Growth

D'ANDRIA Aude, GABARRET Inés
Building 21st Century Entrepreneurship
(Innovation and Technology Set – Volume 2)

DAIDJ Nabyla
Cooperation, Coopetition and Innovation
(Innovation and Technology Set – Volume 3)

FERNEZ-WALCH Sandrine
The Multiple Facets of Innovation Project Management
(Innovation between Risk and Reward Set – Volume 4)

FOREST Joëlle
Creative Rationality and Innovation
(Smart Innovation Set – Volume 14)

GUILHON Bernard
Innovation and Production Ecosystems
(Innovation between Risk and Reward Set – Volume 2)

HAMMOUDI Abdelhakim, DAIDJ Nabyla
Game Theory Approach to Managerial Strategies and Value Creation
(Diverse and Global Perspectives on Value Creation Set – Volume 3)

LALLEMENT Rémi
Intellectual Property and Innovation Protection: New Practices and New Policy Issues
(Innovation between Risk and Reward Set – Volume 3)

LAPERCHE Blandine
Enterprise Knowledge Capital
(Smart Innovation Set – Volume 13)

LEBERT Didier, EL YOUNSI Hafida
International Specialization Dynamics
(Smart Innovation Set – Volume 9)

MAESSCHALCK Marc
Reflexive Governance for Research and Innovative Knowledge
(Responsible Research and Innovation Set – Volume 6)

MASSOTTE Pierre
Ethics in Social Networking and Business 1: Theory, Practice and Current Recommendations
Ethics in Social Networking and Business 2: The Future and Changing Paradigms

MASSOTTE Pierre, CORSI Patrick
Smart Decisions in Complex Systems

MEDINA Mercedes, HERRERO Mónica, URGELLÉS Alicia
Current and Emerging Issues in the Audiovisual Industry
(Diverse and Global Perspectives on Value Creation Set – Volume 1)

MICHAUD Thomas
Innovation, Between Science and Science Fiction
(Smart Innovation Set – Volume 10)

PELLÉ Sophie
Business, Innovation and Responsibility
(Responsible Research and Innovation Set – Volume 7)

SAVIGNAC Emmanuelle
The Gamification of Work: The Use of Games in the Workplace

SUGAHARA Satoshi, DAIDJ Nabyla, USHIO Sumitaka
Value Creation in Management Accounting and Strategic Management: An Integrated Approach
(Diverse and Global Perspectives on Value Creation Set –Volume 2)

UZUNIDIS Dimitri, SAULAIS Pierre
Innovation Engines: Entrepreneurs and Enterprises in a Turbulent World
(Innovation in Engineering and Technology Set – Volume 1)

2016

BARBAROUX Pierre, ATTOUR Amel, SCHENK Eric
Knowledge Management and Innovation
(Smart Innovation Set – Volume 6)

BEN BOUHENI Faten, AMMI Chantal, LEVY Aldo
Banking Governance, Performance And Risk-Taking: Conventional Banks Vs Islamic Banks

BOUTILLIER Sophie, CARRE Denis, LEVRATTO Nadine
Entrepreneurial Ecosystems (Smart Innovation Set – Volume 2)

BOUTILLIER Sophie, UZUNIDIS Dimitri
The Entrepreneur (Smart Innovation Set – Volume 8)

BOUVARD Patricia, SUZANNE Hervé
Collective Intelligence Development in Business

GALLAUD Delphine, LAPERCHE Blandine
Circular Economy, Industrial Ecology and Short Supply Chains (Smart Innovation Set – Volume 4)

GUERRIER Claudine
Security and Privacy in the Digital Era (Innovation and Technology Set – Volume 1)

MEGHOUAR Hicham
Corporate Takeover Targets

MONINO Jean-Louis, SEDKAOUI Soraya
Big Data, Open Data and Data Development (Smart Innovation Set – Volume 3)

MOREL Laure, LE ROUX Serge
Fab Labs: Innovative User (Smart Innovation Set – Volume 5)

PICARD Fabienne, TANGUY Corinne
Innovations and Techno-ecological Transition (Smart Innovation Set – Volume 7)

2015

CASADELLA Vanessa, LIU Zeting, DIMITRI Uzunidis
Innovation Capabilities and Economic Development in Open Economies (Smart Innovation Set – Volume 1)

CORSI Patrick, MORIN Dominique
Sequencing Apple's DNA

CORSI Patrick, NEAU Erwan
Innovation Capability Maturity Model

FAIVRE-TAVIGNOT Bénédicte
Social Business and Base of the Pyramid

GODÉ Cécile
Team Coordination in Extreme Environments

MAILLARD Pierre
Competitive Quality and Innovation

MASSOTTE Pierre, CORSI Patrick
Operationalizing Sustainability

MASSOTTE Pierre, CORSI Patrick
Sustainability Calling

2014

DUBÉ Jean, LEGROS Diègo
Spatial Econometrics Using Microdata

LESCA Humbert, LESCA Nicolas
Strategic Decisions and Weak Signals

2013

HABART-CORLOSQUET Marine, JANSSEN Jacques, MANCA Raimondo
VaR Methodology for Non-Gaussian Finance

2012

DAL PONT Jean-Pierre
Process Engineering and Industrial Management

MAILLARD Pierre
Competitive Quality Strategies

POMEROL Jean-Charles
Decision-Making and Action

SZYLAR Christian
UCITS Handbook

2011

LESCA Nicolas
Environmental Scanning and Sustainable Development

LESCA Nicolas, LESCA Humbert
Weak Signals for Strategic Intelligence: Anticipation Tool for Managers

MERCIER-LAURENT Eunika
Innovation Ecosystems

2010

SZYLAR Christian
Risk Management under UCITS III/IV

2009

COHEN Corine
Business Intelligence

ZANINETTI Jean-Marc
Sustainable Development in the USA

2008

CORSI Patrick, DULIEU Mike
The Marketing of Technology Intensive Products and Services

DZEVER Sam, JAUSSAUD Jacques, ANDREOSSO Bernadette
Evolving Corporate Structures and Cultures in Asia / Impact of Globalization

2007

AMMI Chantal
Global Consumer Behavior

2006

BOUGHZALA Imed, ERMINE Jean-Louis
Trends in Enterprise Knowledge Management

CORSI Patrick *et al.*
Innovation Engineering: the Power of Intangible Networks

www.ingramcontent.com/pod-product-compliance
Lightning Source LLC
LaVergne TN
LVHW012056170926
848329LV00003B/27